T h e
Fiery Serpent

A Christian Theory of Film and Theater

PAUL KURITZ

The
Fiery Serpent

A Christian Theory of Film and Theater

Pleasant Word

A Division of WINEPRESS PUBLISHING

Pleasant Word (a division of WinePress Publishing, PO Box 428, Enumclaw, WA 98022) functions only as book publisher. As such, the ultimate design, content, editorial accuracy, and views expressed or implied in this work are those of the author.

Unless otherwise noted, all Scriptures are taken from the Holy Bible, New International Version, Copyright © 1973, 1978, 1984 by the International Bible Society. Used by permission of Zondervan Publishing House. The "NIV" and "New International Version" trademarks are registered in the United States Patent and Trademark Office by International Bible Society.

Scripture references marked KJV are taken from the King James Version of the Bible.

Scripture references marked NASB are taken from the New American Standard Bible, © 1960, 1963, 1968, 1971, 1972, 1973, 1975, 1977 by The Lockman Foundation. Used by permission.

ISBN 13: 978-1-4141-0767-7
ISBN 10: 1-4141-0767-6
Library of Congress Catalog Card Number: 2006904538

Table of Contents

Preface

In January of 1999 I prayed my first prayer—"Dear God, please don't make me a born-again evangelical Christian." How I came to pray that prayer is the reason I came to write this study.

On the occasion of my fiftieth birthday I decided to follow the example of David Denby, the New York film critic, and reread the books from my first year college course, *The History of Narrative Literature*. I had just read Denby's own account,[1] and my mother's struggle with Alzheimer's Disease convinced me that time for such a project in the future might not be available to me. From memory I constructed the 1966 reading list and began with *The Epic of Gilgamesh*. Then followed *The Iliad* and

The Odyssey in new translations by Robert Fagles, and *The Aeneid*. But then came the Bible.

As a zealous Unitarian I considered skipping that collection of random histories, poetry, and tracts. I had too many other books I knew less about to get on to. But my sense of thoroughness prevailed. Besides, I admired the poetry of the King James Version. So I went to Amazon.com to look for a copy. There I discovered Bibles with footnotes! But since I thought I knew the liberal slant on the Bible, I decided that a conservatively glossed Bible might make a middle-of-the-roader out of me when I finished. I read the reviews and learned that the new *MacArthur Study Bible*[2] had received the most customer raves, so I sent in my $49.95 and waited.

When it arrived, I flipped through with both delight and horror. I liked the "Read through the Bible in a Year" calendar because I could be reading the Bible while moving on to the next books on my list. But when I read the "Overview of Theology," I thought I had made a terrible mistake. How could anyone at the turn of the millennium believe such nonsense! But $49.95 was $49.95, so I began my reading.

Coincidentally, I had been assigned to teach a course I only occasionally taught. The first play of the semester was to be Goethe's *Faust*. I began to prepare my first lectures on the play the same day I began my daily Bible readings. As I considered the German professor's midlife crisis of faith, I noticed that both the Old and New Testament readings in the *MacArthur Study Bible* for the day (and especially the footnotes) tied in very nicely. (For example, right at the beginning of each was Satan making deals.)

The merging of daily Bible readings with the actions in the great play became more acute as the days went on. Characters quoted the scripture I had just read. Scripture and footnotes answered the questions the play's action was raising in my mind. Lectures must have been quite something; students began to bring friends to watch me confront the texts each day.

One Sunday morning, when alone with the mounting coincidences between my readings, I turned on the television and the first words I heard were, "Coincidence is God's way of talking to us." I turned it off immediately. Over the next few days, dropping into random and unrelated listservs on the Internet, I found, "coincidentally," discussions of the very passages I had read that day! Songs on the radio sang the day's words as lyrics! It seemed I couldn't get away from the daily readings. The footnotes in the study Bible offered me the only explanations. I began to hunger after the Word.

After a few months, I thought I was having a breakdown. I was led to read St. Augustine's

Confessions and Pascal's *Pensees*. They were ahead on my list, but who cared. I needed an explanation. I stayed up reading the books, not able to put them down. I recalled that in college they had seemed dull and unfathomable. Now I was riveted by what seemed like transcriptions of what was happening in my mind. I called an old friend, the former chaplain at my school.

When I explained what was going on, he assumed I was joking. I had been the faculty member who volunteered to offer the secular humanist argument to his college Christian student group. Like most of my colleagues, I had a strong mission to erase all superstitions from the young people's minds through education. I was the college Saul persecuting the campus Christians. Eventually, my friend suggested I visit an old friend of his, a counselor at a local hospital. I leaped at the chance! If I were indeed having a breakdown, I could be admitted right away.

The old counselor heard my story and confided that he had been ordained as a conservative evangelical pastor many years before his career in mental health. After about an hour, I asked if he planned on admitting me. He said no, but that he hadn't heard a story like mine in about forty years. When I asked what was wrong, he said I had had a conversion experience! My hope collapsed with an audible, "Oh, no!" What I had assumed was a disorder turned out to be the kingdom of God breaking into my life!

My life was ruined! How could I show my face on a liberal college campus, fraternize with my secular atheist friends, and continue my career in, of all places, the theater? And Christianity could drive my teenage sons away from me. I might as well tattoo my forehead, "I am stupid!" I asked the counselor what kind of a Christian I had become. He said that it sounded like the born-again, evangelical, fundamentalist variety to him. I had become the last thing I ever thought I could become, the last thing I ever wanted to become—a patriotic citizen of the kingdom of God!

Then I prayed my first prayer, "Dear God, please don't make me a born-again evangelical Christian."

And God answered. He said, "No."

I reported the results of my conference to my chaplain friend and again he couldn't believe me. I began to try to convince him. I told him that apparently God knew that only I could convince me and so used His Word and me to that end. I was urged to meet with the campus InterVarsity chaplain. With his encouragement, I eventually told a meeting of the campus Christian group of my experience and the telling became easier, but the shame remained for what I had believed and been for the previous fifty years.

But as I slowly reconciled myself to my new faith, accepting Christ as my savior, Satan attacked. A pastor friend at the Hope Haven Gospel Mission, where I had begun work as a volunteer dishwasher, told me the enemy loved to go after new Christians. Just about everything I had valued in my life was battered and taken away. Scripture and Dottie Rambo's "I Go to the Rock" (my conversion experience had made me like music I previously couldn't abide) kept my head above water during the storms. And as I sang like Paul and Silas, trusting and obeying, the problems subsided, and I was baptized in Harrison, Maine's Crooked River two days before 9/11.

In the kingdom of God I found myself with a peace and joy unlike I had ever even imagined. Christ began to bless me beyond measure. Every aspect of my life began to get better. I had joy in kingdom living.

I had been researching a book for a few years but I couldn't get the topic in focus or the material organized. One summer at a campground meeting, He told me to write the book for Him. In the process, He would reconcile my career in theater and film with my life in the kingdom of God. He was, of course, right. Writing this book has brought me clarity and closeness to my maker.

I have not written for the Christian reader or the non-Christian reader. The Father, the Son, and the Holy Spirit are my audience. I have written to glorify them by writing what I have come to know as the truth about the nature of plays and films as part of the kingdom of God. Whatever is good and true in this book comes from Him. My own work in the dramatic theater has a new priority. My first joy is my duty to God; second comes the privilege of loving my wife, Kathleen; third, I have had delight in fathering my sons, Nathaniel, Ethan, James, and Stefan through the seasons of their young lives.

In Proverbs thirty-one, God paints a picture of the ideal wife and concludes, "Many women have done excellently, but you surpass them all. Charm is deceitful, and beauty is vain, but a woman who fears the Lord is to be praised. Give her of the fruit of her hands, and let her works praise her in the gates." The first time I read that chapter, I thought, *Good luck in finding any woman like that, especially one who would be interested in me!* But the kingdom of God brings blessings that I could never dream to seek. Chief among them is my wife, Kathleen Flynn Kuritz. My son James, himself a new Christian, wisely noted that a man should only marry a woman who will bring him closer to God, and Kathleen has done that and more. She loves the Lord with all her heart, actively seeks the kingdom of God in all things, has a servant heart, and is for me the one God chose from the beginning. She is honest, moral, steadfast, temperate, humorous, wise, loving, and as beautiful outside as she is inside. If my story is my personal proof of God, she is my proof that God loves me. This book and all I do is for God and her.

If reading this book makes you wonder about the kingdom of God and why He created the stage and the screen, please ask the one who has made and directs the great story of which we are all a part. As for me, "I will sing to the Lord as long as I live; I will sing praise to my God while I have my being. May my meditation be sweet to Him; I will be glad in the Lord."[3]

CHAPTER 1

Introduction

The Relationship between Things in Life and Things on the Stage and Screen

The LORD sent fiery serpents among the people and they bit the people, so that many people of Israel died. So the people came to Moses and said, "We have sinned, because we have spoken against the LORD and you; intercede with the LORD, that He may remove the serpents from us." And Moses interceded for the people. Then the LORD said to Moses, "Make a fiery serpent, and get it on a standard; and it shall come about, that everyone who is bitten, when he looks at it, he will live," And Moses made a bronze serpent and set it on the standard; and it came about, that if a serpent bit any man, when he looked to the bronze serpent, he lived.[1]

[Hezekiah] removed the high places and broke down the sacred pillars and cut down the Asherah. He also broke in pieces the bronze serpent that Moses had made, for until those days the sons of Israel burned incense to it; and it was called Nehushtan. He trusted in the LORD, the God of Israel; so that after him there was none like him among all the kings of Judah, nor among those who were before him for he clung to the LORD; he did not depart from following Him, but kept His commandments, which the LORD had commanded Moses, and the LORD was with him; wherever he went he prospered.[2]

What in the world is this peculiar story about? Snake bites? Desperate people seeking relief from their leader? A leader seeking help from God? God interceding in a strange, mysterious, and miraculous way?

It is the story of two realms—the human realm and the supernatural realm, two powers—the power of evil and the power of God, and two ages—the Present Age and the Age to Come. Since exile from paradise, people have been waiting for God to fulfill His promise, to restore His loving rule, and to perfect the relationships within creation. In this story, God breaks into the Present Age–an age dominated by sin, evil, wretchedness, unrighteousness, hatred, deception, strife, conflict, misery, pain, suffering, death, and rebellion against God's will–to temporarily let us see a glimpse and experience a taste of the kingdom of God.[3]

God's Paradigm

The book of Numbers presents God's paradigm for the role of dramatic theater amid the tension between the Present Age and the Age to Come, between the kingdom of men and the kingdom of God. The story demonstrates how the kingdom of God - God's rule or reign - can break through, using human error and sin to both glorify God and bless our lives.

In Numbers chapter twenty-one, we find God's people losing faith in Him and grumbling and complaining about the ways and means God has given them. To draw them back to Him, God allows poisonous snakes to bite and kill His people. In Moses' account in the book of Numbers, the serpents were literal reptiles. They could very well have been metaphors for temptations, leading God's complaining people away from His purpose and their abundant life in Him.

Serpents have been after humans since the Garden of Eden. Snakes trigger something deep in our brains that makes them powerful symbols. In the book of Genesis they are described as the craftiest and most subtle of God's creations. As described by Isaiah, the seraphim, the "fiery serpents," are built into the temple in Jerusalem and fly around the Lord, touching the prophet's mouth with the coal of forgiveness. Serpents are both symbols of great danger and great healing. Two snakes wound around a pillar looking at each other would come to symbolize medicine and medical societies throughout history.

When the Hebrew people put two and two together and realized that their problems were due to their lack of faith in God, they came to Moses and confessed. They asked Moses, God's representative, for help. Moses prayed and God instructed Moses to create something. The healing story of the fiery serpent is a paradigm, not just for medicine but, I believe, for describing God's ability to use the dramatic theater of stage and screen to illustrate the dynamic tension of living simultaneously in two kingdoms, in the Already and in the Not Yet, where His kingdom may burst dramatically into our human world.

Moses was instructed to create a replica of a poisonous snake, to lift it up on a pole, and to isolate it in time and space, for the audience's viewing. God said, "Those who are bitten will live if they simply look at it." Moses did what he was told and those who looked at the snake recovered. How did this happen? How can we begin to understand what was going on?

The Greek philosopher Aristotle held that if we want to know what something is, we need to know four things about it:

- What it is made of
- The form or shape it takes
- The power it needs to come into being
- The end or purpose for which it is made

For example, my sandwich is made of wheat bread, sliced turkey, and mustard. Its form is one piece of bread spread with the mustard, topped by the turkey slices and the second piece of bread. The power of cooking brought it onto my plate, so that it could fulfill its end—provide nourishment for me.

This four-part method of analysis can be applied to anything. For example, we are made mostly of water. We take the form of an integrated body, mind, and soul. The power needed to bring one of us into being is God. The purpose of our life is to glorify our creator and thereby to enjoy life in abundance. We are created, like all made things, in the image of our creator. Critic Brian Godawa notes, "Even though we are fallen, with our art partaking of this fallenness, we are still created in the image of God, and therefore our creations continue to reflect our Maker."[4]

In other words, a made thing has some of the traits of the one who made it. For example, the plays of William Shakespeare reflect his preoccupations, experiences, and style, just as the films of Elia Kazan reflect his. We can begin to understand the creator—Shakespeare or Kazan—by understanding what the creator has made. We can begin to imagine Shakespeare after reading his plays or Elia Kazan after seeing his movies. We can also begin to know God by seeking to know His creation.

One behavior we share with our Creator is the desire and ability to make things so as to make ourselves known to others. Through the fiery serpent God revealed Himself. Through the story of the fiery serpent, God may be revealing His purpose for the dramatic theater.

Dramatic Theater

Art, plays, and movies are ways people make themselves known to others. Ability or skill has been called art, *techne* in Greek. "Art is a fundamental necessity in the human state. 'No man,' says St. Thomas following Aristotle, 'can live without

pleasure. Therefore a man deprived of the pleasures of the spirit goes over to the pleasures of the
flesh.'"[5]

Theater has been defined as the presentation
of oneself or selves, isolated in time and space, to
another or others. *Dramatic theater* has been defined
as the presentation of an imaginary self or selves,
isolated in time and space, to another or others.[6] So
the *art of the dramatic theater* is the ability or skill
of presenting an imaginary self or selves, isolated
in time and space, to another or others. Since some
of us are better able to present an imaginary self
or selves or are more skilled in manipulating the
isolated time and space, some works of dramatic art
are more effective, or better, than others.

What abilities or skills are necessary to create a
work of dramatic theater? Let's use Aristotle's four
questions. The *material* of the dramatic theater is a
human being, isolated in time and space, imagining
before one or more other human beings. Imagining
is picturing in one's mind. The human being imagining is perceived to be imagining when we begin to
share the picturing. Telepathy aside, the imagining
person uses body and voice to communicate what
is happening in his mind. The *form* of dramatic theater is a story, one of our species' defining products.
The *powers* of scriptwriting, acting, directing, and
designing are required so that the dramatic theater
can fulfill its purpose.

All species seek a common *end*: to survive and to reproduce. We are no exception. In fact, the two desires constitute our fundamental happiness. *To survive* means to live without death; a desire for eternal life animates us. *To reproduce* means to leave something of ourselves in our wake. Reproduction is an act of love. (Love is here and throughout defined not as a feeling but as the will to do good, know truth, and experience beauty). Reproduction can partially satisfy our desire to survive. We can reproduce through such things as children, protégés, legacies, and artistic creations. Love is the power for reproduction.

God the creator so loved the Israelite people, that He caused the fiery serpent to be created, lifted up, and endowed with the power to save. Later, to announce the breakthrough of the Age to Come, God the creator so loved the world, His audience, that He initiated the kingdom of God by reproducing Himself as one of them, Jesus Christ, for all of them.

Jesus Christ demonstrated, with signs and wonders, that the kingdom of God, the Age to Come, had finally, in fact, come. By entering into the kingdom through Him, we can experience life in the kingdom of God while still living in the Present Evil Age! This is the story enacted in the birth, death, and resurrection of Jesus Christ for humanity.

All attempts at storytelling and dramatic theater model this historical paradigm—the invasion of the kingdom of God. To the extent that our attempt succeeds, the success resonates across time and space as a universal aesthetic experience-true, good, and beautiful.

Storytelling

Species learn to survive and reproduce through trial and error. Our species has the unique ability to pass on information about surviving and reproducing gleaned by trial and error, through *storytelling*. Great stories climax at a moment, a sign, or a wondrous event, when the kingdom of God breaks in. Storytelling allows us to experience that breakthrough vicariously; it encourages us to expect like breakthroughs in our own lives. Storytelling may even grant fictional accounts the same power to enhance our ability to survive and reproduce as historical accounts.

Dramatic theater that satisfies our yearning for true information, leading to survival and reproduction, makes us happy. We think of that play or film as good, worthy, artful, and beautiful. A good actor has worthy imaginings communicated in artful manipulations of time, space, body, and voice. A good piece of dramatic theater, a true piece of dramatic theater, a beautiful piece of dramatic theater, allows all—maker and audience—to understand life in two kingdoms, to seek more of the kingdom of God, to understand and love God, oneself, and our fellow human beings more than before.

Our universal desire for survival and reproduction can, in the hands of this Evil Age, result in plays and movies awash in sex and violence, the crudest means of achieving our desires. In fact, dramatic theater's makers have often imagined our basest instincts on the stage because, as long as we remain trapped in this Present Age, we are subject to the desires of the flesh. Stories often show us seeking the world's kingdom, conforming to this Evil Age, rejecting the kingdom of God even after experiencing the blessings of its breakthrough.

The Form of the Serpent

The shape or form of the fiery serpent was drawn from the personal experiences of the people; the serpents were real everyday serious problems. The fiery serpent on the pole looked like a real serpent to its audience. But the bronze serpent did not pose a threat to the people; they were able to contemplate it without fear. The bronze serpent was harmless due to the material of which it was made.

The serpent was also more than just a serpent lifted up. The serpent had been transformed. The serpent was a preview of the future great lifting up of Christ, the human incarnation of the kingdom of God. The serpent alone could not accomplish what it accomplished. But because the serpent was conceived and created by God in the shadow of the cross of Christ as a prelude to the arrival of His kingdom, the work of art attained its transcendent power.

The Material of the Serpent

The material of the fiery serpent was bronze, not the tissues that make an actual serpent. Bronze is an alloy made when two less precious metals, copper-bearing rock and tin, are heated by charcoal fire. The molten metal was poured into a cast or mold of a serpent. When cooled and hardened, the bronze form was filed and polished.

The Power to Make the Serpent

To make a bronze serpent required the God-given *techne*, or skill, of the artist. Skill, innate or learned, comes from God; the Lord fills the artist "with the Spirit of God, with skill, with intelligence, with knowledge, and with all craftsmanship, to devise artistic designs."[7] Skill is a mysterious gift, a product of an invasion by the kingdom of God.

The Purpose of the Serpent

God provided the skill to make the bronze serpent. God also provided the purpose of the fiery serpent—to glorify God by doing what we could not do, namely, to save ourselves from death. How can that which brings death—snakes—bring life? Through a transformative process originating in the Age to Come. By seeking God's will for the art, the artist produced a work with both kingdom power and practical human value. God crowned the work, made the bronze look like fire, and attracted the audience to the light it reflected. The work reflected God's transcendent and transformative light because every aspect of the work—form, material, manner, and purpose—reflected God's kingdom purpose and glory.

As a result of this God-glorifying work of art, the people were saved from death, restored to health, and shown the kingdom of God, where they might enjoy their abundant lives in God. How does it work? God's will, His Word, and His almighty grace are sufficient. The artists seek, God provides. *The Wisdom of Solomon* summarizes the story:

Even when the fearful rage of wild animals
overtook them
And they were perishing from the bites of
writhing snakes,
Your retribution did not continue to the end.
Affliction struck them briefly, by way of
warning,
And they had a saving token to remind them of
the commandment of your Law,
For whoever turned to it was saved, not by
what he looked at,
But by you, the Savior of all.
And by such means you proved to our enemies
That you are the one who delivers from every
evil;
For them, the bites of locusts and flies proved
fatal
and no remedy could be found to save their
lives,
since they deserved to be punished by such
creatures.
But your children,
Not even the fangs of poisonous snakes could
bring them down;
For your mercy came to their help and cured
them.
One sting–how quickly healed!–
To remind them of your pronouncements

Rather than that, by sinking into deep
forgetfulness,
They should be cut off from your kindness.
No herb, no poultice cured them,
But your all-healing word, Lord.[8]

Christian dramatic theater—the fiery serpent—is the gospel of grace, a mysterious invasion of the kingdom of God into our Evil Age, an imitation of our Lord Jesus Christ. "And just as Moses lifted up the serpent in the desert on a pole, so must the Son of Man be lifted up" (John 3:14). That the Lord should be symbolized by a dead serpent!

The paradigmatic story in Numbers presents the model for our dramatic theater makers who seek to imitate the means and ends of the great maker Himself. As the psalmist proclaimed, "Great are the works of the Lord; They are studied by all who delight in them."[9] Dramatic theater can present the story of a human being trapped in this Evil Age, confronted by a breakthrough into his life by the kingdom of God. He chooses to accept or reject the effects of that invasion. If accepted, he may be healed or restored. He may or may not acknowledge the kingdom of God as the source of his blessing. If made for the purpose of glorifying God, the film or play can have the ability to invite us into the kingdom of God. At least, the work can cause us to reconsider the kingdom in which we live and the gods which we serve.

Many works of the dramatic theater glorify humanity. In a later episode of the story, King Hezekiah destroys the work of art when the work became valued for itself rather than for the God who infused every aspect of its creation; who made the bronze look like fire. The young king destroys Moses' bronze serpent because the people had begun to worship and glorify the serpent rather than the source of the serpent's healing power.

Art for art's sake, or even for society's or people's sake, is idolatry. Dramatic theater which is made and loved for itself rather than as a means of glorifying the creator, the source of the dramatic theater's power, is likewise not as effective in moving, healing, or blessing us. God wants art to be made and enjoyed for His sake. Plays and films are not for dramatic theater's sake, not even for our sake, but for the sake of, for the glory of the creator, the giver and sustainer of our lives. Only then can they have kingdom value and power. As Hamlet concludes, there must be acknowledgement of the kingdom of God— what he calls "a Providence which shapes our ends" —in the dramatic theater, as in our lives.

Films and plays have shown people living outside the kingdom of God, experiencing meaninglessness, except for what they can convince themselves has meaning. Yet even when the kingdom of God breaks through, human rule is not immediately or totally overthrown. The kingdom comes as an offer. God does not compel people to rid themselves of problems, temptations, or death by forced membership in His kingdom. But He does provide the miraculous invitation, as He did with the fiery serpent and with the cross.

As the truth of the kingdom of God informs the dramatic theater, God points us to Christ. God does not establish the kingdom of God in or through the dramatic theater, but He uses it to show its power, to awaken our desire to seek it, to deepen our trust in God, to empower us to live in the kingdom of God safely and without fear in a world of poisonous snakes, sex, violence, and temptation. The Christian dramatic theater, like the fiery serpent, is a glimpse of grace, leading us to the source of grace. Christian films and plays point the way to the kingdom of God; they do not remove all our fears, or take away the pain of the snakebite. But they invite us to travel in the kingdom of God.

The creation of films or plays is only a worthy endeavor because God is the creator. We can only create because we are made in the image of our creator. No other species was made in the creator's image. Consequently, no other creature can create like we can.

God is the power that brings about human beings. To bring His kingdom power to bear on our endeavor called dramatic theater, He must be glorified. He must be the chief audience member whose approval the artists' imaginings seek. But unlike God, we can only make out of something already made; only God can create from nothing. Without God's initial creation, we would have nothing to use in our creations. God created us to reflect His godly behaviors back to Him. We create to reflect our God-given human behaviors back to God in appreciation, and to His glory.

Films and plays can narrate several basic stories of the Christian world view. First, the story can depict fallen man, lost and depraved, revolting against God, conforming to this Evil Age. These heroes live with faith in the things of the earth—themselves, others, wealth, political philosophy, knowledge, or pleasure. A second basic story reveals men's confrontation with an invasion of the kingdom of God into their lives. Unfulfilled and empty outside the kingdom, the fallen and flawed heroes may eventually find redemption, outside of themselves and their world, in the kingdom of God. In some stories the hero chooses to remain as he is; in others, he decides to seek the kingdom of God. Sometimes we see a hero living in the tension of life in both worlds. An encounter with the Already/Not Yet Kingdom causes the hero to reconsider his view of the world, if only for a moment.

In comedies, audiences can laugh at and ridicule heroes whose faith in this Evil Age is either excessive or defective, who never question the objects of their misplaced faith. In tragedies, audiences can pity heroes who find themselves in fearful situations of betrayal by that to which they have given their faith. In melodramas and tragicomedies, heroes may be rescued by a breakthrough of God's kingdom. The heroes may either seek the kingdom of God or rationalize away their unusual encounter, and thereby continue to misplace their faith.

The Christian plot defies the classical definitions of comedy and tragedy by transcending each, with heroes free from both death and public opinion. Redemption is the arc of the action in the Christian story. We see a person enjoy the blessings of the Age to Come, even while remaining in this Evil Age. We see the blessings God's kingdom grants its inhabitants, even while they continue to live in the fallen world. We see a person yield to the rule of the kingdom of God. We see a person seek the righteousness of the kingdom. We see the indwelling Holy Spirit impart new life. As Jacques Maritain notes, "The definition of Christian art is to be found in its subject and its spirit...It is the art of humanity redeemed."[10] Redemption necessitates the discovery of the truth of Christ, "I am the Way, the Truth, and the Life."[11] Truth is a person who rules the kingdom of God; His name is Jesus.

The human mind does not think truth; it encounters truth. Our universal ability to understand certain dramatic plots, stories, characters, and thoughts suggests the universality of the concepts the words and images represent. Just as our senses detect real shapes and colors, so our minds detect real harmonies and unities in plays and films. After the initial shock of the new wears off, beneath the play's or film's cultural and individual differences we begin to find universal concepts which make appreciation and translation possible. Beneath different cultural customs and mores lie common human values and aesthetic desires. The similarities among Sanskrit drama, Noh theater, Shakespeare, and Broadway musicals are massive; far greater than their differences. The differences are usually differences in emphasis, not wholly new aesthetic systems. Aesthetic disagreements in the history of the film and drama are just about matters of degree. A completely new aesthetic cannot be imagined any more than a completely new color.

Our mind can create the rules of soccer and chess and can change them. The rules aren't there until we make them. But our mind discovers other universal rules given by God. Such rules affect the dramatic theater. We can't change the God imprinted rules.

They are natural to our humanity. The universal existence of nonconformists and rebels proves the presence of a natural aesthetic that transcends particular societies. We may be free to create plotless stories, without humanly recognizable characters. But we are not free from our innate instinct to assume a story involving beings with human traits in what we are witnessing. The events of a play or film may be chosen by random selection but we will project causality onto what we see. We may seek to create a meaningless play or film, but we cannot stop our desire to find meaning; even meaninglessness is a meaning. We are made to seek meaning.

This book investigates the nature and art of the dramatic theater—movies and plays—through a Christian lens. These basic questions will seem familiar to readers versed in the inquiries of Aristotle, St. Augustine, and St. Thomas Aquinas:

- What is the relationship between things in life and things on the stage and screen?
- What is the Material Cause of the dramatic theater?
- What are the natural materials used to make dramatic theater?
- How does it compare to God's Material Cause in creation?

- What is the Formal Cause of the dramatic theater?
- What blueprint does the dramatic theater follow? What is the architectonic element of the dramatic theater?
- What is its relationship to the shape God gave creation?
- What is the function of storytelling? For God? For humans? For theater artists?
- What are human traits? Where do they come from? How do they compare to the behaviors of characters in the dramatic theater?
- What is the relationship between the words of a script or screenplay and the Word?
- What is the relationship of the dramatic theater to ideas like art and beauty?
- What is beauty in the dramatic theater?
- What makes a play or film beautiful?
- What is goodness in the dramatic theater?
- What makes a play or film good?
- What makes a good work of dramatic theater?
- What is truthfulness in the dramatic theater?
- What makes a truthful play or film?
- What is the Efficient Cause of the dramatic theater?

- What power causes a work of dramatic theater to come into being?
- What is its relationship to the power which causes creation?
- What is the Final Cause of the dramatic theater?
- What is the purpose of the dramatic theater?
- How does it relate to God's purpose in creation?
- What does it mean to be a Christian working in the theater and film?
- What is it like to be a Christian theater artist?
- What ought it to be like to be a Christian theater artist?
- What purpose does God have for a Christian theater artist?

CHAPTER 2

The Formal Cause of the Dramatic Theater

The Architectonic Component of the Dramatic Theater and Its Relationship to the Shape God Gave Creation

In the beginning was the Word, and the Word was with God, and the Word was God. He was in the beginning with God; all things were made through him, and without him was not anything made that was made. In him was life, and the life was the light of men. The light shines in the darkness, and the darkness has not overcome it. And the Word became flesh and dwelt among us,

full of grace and truth; we have beheld his glory,
glory as of the only Son from the Father.

—John 1:1-5,14 RSV

The Word of God is the story of God's dynamic relationship with His creation. The story is the form of God's revealed word. God is the original storyteller. In the Bible's story of God in relationship with human beings, He is the star; we are the supporting players. Robert McKee says, "Storytelling is the creative demonstration of truth. A story is the living proof of an idea, the conversion of an idea to action. A story's event structure is the means by which you first express, then prove, your idea…without explanation."[1] God revealed His truth through men inspired by the Holy Spirit to write His story in human words. God's idea is His love for His creation.

Story

If a story is the form of both God's revelation and of the dramatic theater, then what is a story? A *story* is an ordering of events through a beginning, a middle, to an ending, which follows a main character through his struggle to achieve a certain goal. A stage play is a story told in words and pictures; a film is a story told in pictures and words. Film director Howard Hawks maintained, "a good director is a good storyteller."[2] Director Mel Gibson agrees:

"I'm doing what I've always done: telling stories I think are important in the language I speak best: film. I think most great stories are hero stories. People want to reach out and grab at something higher, and vicariously live through heroism, and lift their spirit that way."[3]

An image like the bronze serpent reflects light onto the audience's retinas. This creates the sensation that something is happening in us. Then we have a perception that something is happening out there due to the work of a dramatic artist. And Nicholas Humphrey states, that "although too little is known to be sure, there are good grounds for supposing that the sensory channel makes use of 'analog' processing and ends up with a pictorial representation (something like a picture in the brain), while the perceptual channel makes use of 'digital' processing and ends up with a prepositional representation (more like a description in words)."[4]

While both film and plays involve pictures and words, each gravitates to a particular characteristic channel. Film is pictures; the sensory channel is the foundation of film. Plays are words; the perception channel is the foundation of plays. Humphrey continues: "The process of perceptual representation has to involve something more like making up a story about what this stimulus signifies to be occurring in the outside world."[5]

A story is, according to Donald Hall, "any development…by chronological order."[6] Life is a chronological story because it exists in time and space. As the writer G. K. Chesterton notes, "I had always felt life first as a story; and if there is a story there is a storyteller."[7] God wrote the script: "According to most philosophers, God, in making the world, enslaved it. According to Christianity, in making it, He set it free. God had written, not so much a poem, but rather a play; a play he had planned as perfect, but which had necessarily been left to human actors and stage managers, who had since made a great mess of it."[8]

Structure

The ordering of events through a beginning to the end creates a structure. The beginning of the story is the part where we find out who and what the story is about, who is the main character, and what is the problem. In His story, God is the main character, and our belief that we are the main characters, is the problem. In the middle of a story, the main character wants something, but can't get it—things or people stand in the way. God wants an intimate, joyous relationship with us, but cannot have it because we continue to rely on ourselves rather than on Him to find joy. As the middle of a story develops, the obstacles become greater and more difficult to overcome until the story reaches the climax. At the turning points of His story, God enters His story. The kingdom of God breaks into the human kingdom as God works to save us from ourselves. The end of a story includes the climax and resolution: Is the protagonist's goal achieved? What are the consequences?

God's story is complete, but since we are in it, we can only anticipate the ending and consequences God has promised. We, in the middle, either do not know how soon the end will come, or realize the end has begun with the birth, death, and resurrection of Jesus Christ. The kingdom of this earth has become the kingdom of our God. The anticipated End of Days has arrived.

As we continue to face problems, we echo Frodo and Sam in *The Lord of the Rings*: "You and I, Sam, are stuck in the worst part of the story, and it is all too likely that some will say at this point: 'Shut the book now, dad; we don't want to read any more' 'Maybe', said Sam, 'but I wouldn't want to be one to say that. Things done and over and made into part of the great tales are different.'"[9] We know the victory is ours. We see His signs and wonders. We experience His blessings.

Storytelling and story hearing are features unique to our species. They are the basis for the organization of the dramatic theater's actions. All stories that hold our interest have the same parts, whether written two thousand years ago or yesterday, whether written in Sanskrit or Ebonics. Every story progresses from a beginning, through a middle, to an end. The dramatic theater artist is a skilled maker of represented narratives, whether for the stage or for the screen.

As the apostle John writes, "In the beginning was the Word, and the Word was..." The great story, the story of God and the breakthrough of His kingdom in the life, death, and resurrection of Jesus Christ, echoes in all people, at all times, and in all places. Every person, family, and culture has pieces of this story that resonate as the truth when they hear it.

The capacity to hear and understand His story is hardwired in our souls. Christ figures are perceived in a wide variety of stories, regardless of their authors' intent. The incarnation of Christ is a mystery, but Christ figures on stage and screen help us explore the humanity of a person whose life mirrors Christ's in some way. Director James Cameron created a trilogy of Christ figures in his sci-fi films *The Abyss, Aliens,* and the *Terminator* series. Christ figures have been found in films as diverse as *Metropolis, Open City, Casablanca, Mr. Smith Goes to*

Washington, *High Noon*, *The Iron Giant*, *Meet John Doe*, *Goodbye*, *Mr. Chips*, *One Against the Wind*, *Being There*, *E.T.*, *The Mission*, *The Shawshank Redemption*, *Babette's Feast*, *Breaking the Waves*, *Glory*, *Ghandi*, *Spitfire Grill*, *Schindler's List*, *We Were Soldiers*, *Braveheart*, *Phenomenon*, *The Bridge on the River Kwai*, *The Great Escape*, *To Sir With Love*, *Bagdad Café*, *Sling Blade*, *Dead Man Walking*, and *On the Waterfront*, and in plays as diverse as *Oedipus Rex*, *The Devil's Disciple*, *Who's Afraid of Virginia Woolf?*, *The Glass Menagerie*, *A Man for All Seasons*, *The Miracle Worker*, and *Hamlet*. The director of *On the Waterfront* explains,

> Yes, the story is strong and well put together, and there is a lot of violence and a love story, and there are even a few laughs, and sure everyone likes to see the underdog come out on top–but three hundred people before the box office has opened? What is it they smelled? My guess is that it's the theme, that of a man who has sinned and is redeemed…Budd Schulberg struck a deep human craving there: redemption for a sinner, rescue from damnation. Redemption, isn't that the promise of the Catholic Church?…There are gut reasons like that for the success of the great hits. They touch a fundamental hunger in people. Yes, that a man can, no matter what he's done, be redeemed.[10]

Every Christ figure, like every main character, lives in an orderly three-part structure, referred to either as problem, complication, and resolution, or as exposition, complication, and denouement. The three-part structure is evident in both *Hamlet* and *On the Waterfront*. Director Tom Shadyac notes that problems and complications are essential to storytelling: "We are storytellers. And as storytellers we are dealing with human actors, people, writers, characters. And humans, as you know, tend to make mistakes…Jesus was a storyteller. He didn't get into a lot of dogma when he told the story of the Prodigal Son…"[11]

Structure is, according to Syd Field, "the force that holds everything together; it is the skeleton, the spine, the foundation. Without structure, you have no story."[12] "The root *struct* means 'to put together.' Simply put, structure is the relationship between the parts and the whole."[13]

Unity

The parts include plot, characters, action, dialogue, scenes, sequences, incidents, and events. A story is divided into moments or sequences, according to how each fits into the overall story, the reason for its being where it is. Films are sequences of scenes, of shots, of movements, and of lines of words.

Stage plays are acts of scenes, of units of action, of movements, and of lines of words. Unity requires a reason for each element being where it should be. Dorothy Sayers notes, "quite simply, every choice of an episode, or a phrase, or a word is made to conform to a pattern of the entire [work], which is revealed by that choice as already existing."[14]

A script's structure approaches *unity* as the whole contains nothing extraneous. A unified structure has a coherent sequence of events presented from a consistent viewpoint. Elia Kazan observed that, "a screenplay's worth has to be measured less by its language than by its architecture and how that dramatizes the theme. A screenplay, we directors soon enough learn, is not a piece of writing as much as it is a construction. We learn to feel for the skeleton under the skin of words."[15]

A unified story must have enough detail so we know what is happening but not so much that we get lost. The director of *On the Waterfront* echoes these sentiments: "Budd and I wished we had been able to go deeper into the social structure, which supports the gangsters. On the other hand, if we had gone more into that, we would have lost some of the unity of the film."[16]

In creation, order is everywhere. Extraordinarily complex and multi-layered arrangements that imply an intelligence and purpose are evident everywhere.

Solomon noted that in creation "there is nothing to add to it and there is nothing to take from it."[17] "He has made everything appropriate in its time."[18] The pioneer film director Allan Dwan sought mathematical unity: "Stories, to me, were mathematical problems–as most problems were. There's always a mathematical solution to anything."[19] Dwan looked for geometrical perfection in relationships:

> Everything I did was triangles with me. If I constructed a story and I had four characters in it, I'd put them down as dots and if they didn't hook up into triangles, if any one of them were left dangling out there without a sufficient relationship to any of the rest, I knew I had to discard them because they'd be a distraction. And you're only related to people through triangles or lines. If I'm related to a third person and you're not, there's something wrong in our relationship together. One of us is dangling. So I say, "How do I tie that person to you? How do I complete that line?" And I have to work the story so I can complete that line. In other words, create a relationship, an incident, something that will bring us into the eternal triangle.[20]

If we were to find a script or camera or projector in the woods, we would quickly, and without a moment's hesitation, assume two things: first, it belonged to someone and second, it had been made. Why would we assume it was made? Because of its complex, orderly, and purposeful arrangement of parts.

God constructs our existence the way a screen-writer or playwright constructs action. Each "gives to all things what is right, defining proportion, beauty, order, arrangement, and all dispositions of place and rank for each, in accordance with that place which is most truly right."[21] The screenwriter's story affects even the smallest actions by the actor. Alfred Hitchcock explains: "I talk to [the actors] and explain to them what the scene is, what its purpose is, why they are doing certain things—because they relate to the story, not to the scene. The whole scene relates to the story but that little look does this or that for the story."[22]

The unity of the structure requires proportion of design. Chesterton notes, "Proportion cannot be adrift: it is either an accident or a design."[23] God is an omnipotent and omniscient designer, while the theater and film artist is limited in ability and knowledge. Nevertheless, both designers employ recurring patterns and variations; "pattern and variation are interdependent concepts fundamental to art."[24] Jonathan Witt states, "The artist seeks variety within unity, rhythm, and harmony, qualities fundamental to the creation of beauty."[25] "Ought we to demote

Monet from the first rank of the impressionists because he had the bad taste to paint poplars and haystacks over and over again? Do we not instead marvel at the fecundity of his imagination, at the subtly of his observation and insight?"[26] "No one, not even his harshest eighteenth century critics, accuses Shakespeare of bad art on the grounds that *Much Ado about Nothing* and *Othello* share virtually the same plot, creatively altered to produce radically different plays. Few if any object to Shakespeare's repetition of motherless girls as heroines, or to his girls-disguised-as-boys theme, or to his repetitive use of the sonnet form for his poetry."[27]

The Beginning

In creation, God brings matter into the form of a story from nothing. In making a script, on the other hand, the writer orders and transforms existing matter—personal experience—according to a plan or idea in his imaginative mind. As nature is not created in any other way than according to God's plan, art is not produced any way but according to one's intelligence. Both creation and dramatic theater are carefully organized. As biologist Edward O. Wilson observed, "Nature is organized by simple universal laws of physics to which all other laws and principles can eventually be reduced."[28]

If there are any scientific laws that have universal acceptance, and universal applicability, they are the laws of thermodynamics. Thermodynamics literally means "energy in action." The first law of thermodynamics may be stated thus: energy can neither be created nor destroyed. If it is true, then neither energy, nor matter, can be created from nothing, except by God. The law gives credence to the Law of Causality: every effect has a cause.

The second law of thermodynamics builds upon the first. The second law states that heat will not pass spontaneously to a warmer body. Other ways of stating the law could be:

- The improbable rarely happens.
- Entropy (disorder) increases.
- Entropy is the arrow of time; chronology moves from order to disorder.

The laws have wide implications. For example, imagine you are watching a film of waves lapping a beach and as they recede a sandcastle slowly rises up from the flat sand. The sandcastle was an unexpected order among the disorder of the beach. The sandcastle is also unlikely, so another, and better, definition of entropy might be *likelihood*. In creation, entropy always increases, so the film must be running backwards.

There is only one exception to this law in creation—God's exception. God can break into this world and the improbable happens, or disorder decreases, or chronology is upended. Life itself is a violation of natural laws. Life is God's kingdom breaking into the kingdom of decay. Life is decreasing entropy. Life builds up the improbable structure of its cells from the disordered materials around it. It does this, however, at the expense of increasing the entropy around it, and it always eventually decays back to the disorder from which it came. Another statement of the second law is that entropy, or randomness, is constantly increasing.

There are important dramatic, philosophic, and religious implications in the laws of thermodynamics. If the laws are true, and have always been true, then the universe has always existed. If this is true, and has always been true, then by this time it would have achieved complete entropy. The only explanation for the lack of complete entropy is that the laws of thermodynamics haven't always been true. Why not? Because there were interventions by God; breakthroughs by the kingdom of God that created something from nothing, as the trigger which created the universe.

The universe had a definite beginning. There was a time when it did not exist, when God brought it into being. Likewise, a play or a film has not always existed. A maker brings them into being "in the beginning." In the beginning, something happens that sets off the series of linked episodes. Director Leo McCarey had a theory, "which I call the ineluctability of incidents. The idea is that if something happens, some other thing inevitably flows from it—like night following day; events are linked together. I always develop my stories that way, in a series of incidents that succeed and provoke each other."[29]

One feature of a story that separates it from all other types of account is the quality of "specialness." Ellen Dissanayake notes that "the faculty for making and expressing specialness" actually differentiates art from other things.[30] Life is special because it is the story of God intervening into human life with signs and wonders. Likewise, plays and films are special. *On the Waterfront* occurs the day a beloved brother "falls" off a roof. *Hamlet* occurs on the heels of two special events—the death of the king and the remarriage of the queen. *A Midsummer Night's Dream* is framed by the special wedding of fairy royalty, Oberon and Titania. *A Doll's House* opens on Christmas Eve. The premiere of Constantin's new play distinguishes the occasion of *The Seagull*. And today is the day Godot actually arrives in Beckett's *Waiting for Godot*. Stories are made special by their occasions; Ellen Dissanayake notes that "making important activities special has been basic and fundamental to human evolution and existence."[31]

Trigger events occur early in a story's beginning. As the apostle John begins, "In the beginning was the Word, and the Word was with God, and the Word was God." God has always had company in the person of the *Logos*. In the beginning of His story, God, in relationship with Himself, decided to create; all things were created through the personal and relational *Logos*. Apart from *Logos* nothing came into being. *Logos* is God's creative utterance of the Old Testament; George Steiner points out, "in the Hebraic perspective, creation is a rhetoric, a literal speech-act...The *ruah Elohim*, the breath or *pneuma* of the Creator speaks the world."[32] God's utterance, the trigger event, the initial act issuing from the kingdom of God, is the effective cause of life. Some scientists point to this "big bang" to mark the onset of God's story. *Logos* is God acting, doing, making, and creating. *Logos* is God's agent for action, for animating and maintaining life. As J. I. Packer notes, "Created things do not have life in themselves, but life in the Word, the second person of the Godhead."[33] *Logos* was the light, illuminating and revealing both human life, and the God who created it.

The Middle

The middle is the bulk of the story. During the middle two forces work in opposition so that conflict arises. All conflict ultimately arises from the great conflict—the kingdom of this world against the kingdom of God, the power of evil versus the power of God, and the Present Age resisting the Age to Come. Robert McKee[34] has outlined certain principles about story which are both evident in God's story, and hallmarks of all effective human dramatic stories:

- Story is about principles, not rules.
- Story is about eternal, universal forms, not formulas.
- Story is about archetypes, not stereotypes.
- Story is about thoroughness, not shortcut.
- Story is about respect, not disdain, for the audience.
- Story is about originality, not duplication.

Like God's story, our stories are about relationships: the relationship between us and God, our family, our culture, and our surroundings. The dramatic theater, on stage and screen, often reveals the consequences of separation, alienation, and estrangement in relationships. There are four basic conflicts:

- Man versus God
- Man versus nature
- Man versus man
- Man versus himself

Man versus himself is an internal conflict. The most common conflict is man versus man: the old Adam in this Present Age versus a new life through Christ in the Already/Not Yet kingdom of God. Every conflict involves a moment at a crossroads that hinges on a decision: Who rules my life? To whom do I owe allegiance? Whose kingdom will I seek? In what do I have faith? Chesterton observes, "All Christianity concentrates on the man at the crossroads…Will a man take this road or that? That is the only thing to think about, if you enjoy thinking."[35] The writer Walker Percy noted the special nature of the Christian story:

> I am speaking of the mystery of human life, its sense of predicament, of something having gone wrong, as life as a wayfaring and a pilgrimage, of the density and linearity of time and the sacramental reality of things. The intervention of God in history through the Incarnation bestows a weight and value to the individual human narrative which is like money in the bank to the [writer]. Sin is out of fashion, both with Christians and with Jews, let alone unbelievers.

But any [writer] who does not believe that his
character finds himself in a predicament not entirely of his own making or of society's making is
in trouble...and any [writer] who begins...with
his character in a life predicament which is a
profound mystery to which he devotes his entire
life to unraveling...is a closet Jew or Christian
whether he likes it or not.[36]

In the middle of God's story, *Logos* did something
incomprehensible: it invaded this Evil Age to declare
its rule and sovereignty. To restore His world and
our relationship with Him, *Logos* incarnated itself
in human form! The Word of God became the Son
of God. And the Son of God is God Himself in human form, proclaiming the arrival of the kingdom
of God, demonstrating its power with signs and
wonders, and inviting all to enter in. God became
a character: the saving, suffering hero, in His own
script. Marshall McLuhan comments:

I suggest that our faith in the Incarnation has
an immediate relevance to our art, science, and
philosophy. Since the Incarnation all men have
been taken up into the poetry of God, the Divine
Logos, the Word, His Son. But Christians alone
know this. And knowing this, our own poetry,
our own power of incarnating and uttering the
world, becomes a precious foretaste of the Divine

> Incarnation and the Evangel. We can see how all
> things have been literally fulfilled in Christ, espe-
> cially our powers of perception. And in Christ we
> can look more securely and steadfastly on natural
> knowledge which at one and the same time has
> become easier and also less important to us.[37]

Likewise in the middle of their story, dramatic characters meet the kingdom of God, with more freedom, more justice, and a change in all their relationships. The hero catches a peek of the nature of the kingdom of God. Derek Morphew suggests "its power is already present in an unexpected intervention of God so we can say that it is actually present, but its presence is not exhaustive. The mysterious nature of the kingdom of God consists of the fact that it is always here, almost here, delayed, and future."[38] Think of Hamlet after his "chance" discovery of the letter at sea! Think of *On the Waterfront* and of Edie Boyle, away from the safety of her convent, breaking into longshoreman Terry Malloy's life with a slap! When these unlikely lives receive the Spirit, however unwillingly, they experience the power of the Age to Come. As a result, Hamlet and Terry lose interest in their past and present situations as they orient their actions to the future possibilities of their lives. The transformed characters live in expectation of more breakthroughs, not through their deeds, but through the grace of God.

Freedom and Limitation

Chesterton claims "a story is exciting because it has in it so strong an element of will, of what theology calls free will."[39] This is the paradox of both life and the dramatic theater. How can a person or character, whose next action is scripted, act freely? How can free will live within the limitations of a structured order?

"Art is limitation; the essence of every picture is the frame."[40] The characters in a play or film are not free after they are made. They only appear to be so. In the making of a stage play or film the actors convince themselves that they are totally free to act upon any decision. They willingly suspend their disbelief. They put their next lines and actions so far from their conscious minds that they convince themselves that they are not following a script! C. S. Lewis explains:

> Suppose I am writing a [script]. I write "Mary laid down her work; next moment came a knock at the door!" For Mary who has to live in the imaginary time of my story there is no interval between putting down the work and hearing the knock. But I, who am Mary's maker, do not live in that imaginary time at all. Between writing the first half of that sentence and the second, I might sit down for three hours and think steadily about

Mary. I could think about Mary as if she were the only character in the [script] and for as long as I pleased, and the hours I spent in doing so would not appear in Mary's time (the time inside the [script]) at all.

This is not a perfect illustration, of course. But it may give just a glimpse of what I believe to be the truth. God is not hurried along in the time-stream of this universe any more than an author is hurried along in the imaginary time of his own [script]. He has infinite attention to spare for each one of us. He does not have to deal with us in the mass. You are as much alone with Him as if you were the only being He had ever created. When Christ died, He died for you individually as much as if you had been the only man in the world.[41]

Like us, actors at work need and flourish within limitations. Lewis continues, "The artist loves his limitations: they constitute the thing he is doing…. The moment you step into the world of facts, you step into a world of limits. You can free things from accidental or alien laws, but not from the laws of their own nature…A man cannot expect any adventures in the land of anarchy. But a man can expect any number of adventures if he goes traveling in the land of authority. One can find no meanings in a jungle of skepticism; but the man will find more and more meanings who walks through a forest of doctrine and design. Here everything has a story tied to its tail."[42]

The End

The story of the screenwriter or playwright unfolds according to his arrangement of the incidents so that the writer's intention will be realized at the conclusion of the film or play. Because of the expectations and probabilities established in the middle of a story, every end presents the possibility of reconciliation, restoration, and redemption, as an individual seeks to deny, forget, renew, or establish relationships. Lewis adds, "To the Buddhist or the eastern fatalist existence is a science or a plan, which must end up in a certain way. But to a Christian, existence is a story which may end up in any way."[43]

The universal truth underlying the arc of the drama is the possibility of a happy ending—redemption or salvation through Christ. As critic Brian Godawa notes, "Movie storytelling is about redemption—the recovery of something lost or the attainment of something needed."[44] If this is true, then certain other endings are unhappy, and certain thoughts and ideas are false. The Christian dramatic theater can demonstrate the falseness of other, competing, and tempting ideas such as salvation through knowledge; human ignorance as the source of evil; the plurality of beliefs; human responsibility for pain; the relativity of good and evil; or ethics as a means of redemption.

While words constitute the beginning of creation, they can also be the final element in the construction of a script. Director Alfred Hitchcock explains his method:

> I would always work on a treatment with a writer who would be a plot maker, or a story man. I would work weeks and weeks on this treatment, and what it would amount to would be a complete narrative, even indicating shots, but not in the words of a long shot or close-up. I would have everything in it, all the details. Then I used to give it to a top writer to do the dialog. When he sent in his dialog, I would sit down and dictate the shots in a complete continuity. But the film had to be made on paper in this narrative form. It would describe the film, shot by shot, beginning to end.[45]

Words

The theater artist imitates the formal process of God with his story. The playwright and screenwriter have an ongoing relationship with their words. In fact, the writer can only be known through his words. C.S. Lewis noted the relationship between words and pictures, "It is of the very nature of thought and language to represent what is immaterial in picturable terms."[46] All things made by the scriptwriter come through his words. Words bring the author into existence; the scriptwriter's words bring the story to life. Pope John Paul II stated,

> In producing a work, artists express themselves to the point where their work becomes a unique disclosure of their own being, of what they are and of how they are what they are. And there are endless examples of this in human history. In shaping a masterpiece, the artist not only summons his work into being, but also in some way reveals his own personality by means of it. For him art offers both a new dimension and an exceptional mode of expression for his spiritual growth. Through his works, the artist speaks to others and communicates with them. The history of art, therefore, is not only a story of works produced, but also a story of men and women. Works of great art speak of their authors; they enable us to know their inner life, and they reveal the original contribution which artists offer to the history of culture.[47]

The dramatic theater writer's words call forth human beings to embody the words. Actors-as-characters are the screenwriter's words made flesh. The words of the script become the actors-as-characters. And the actors-as-characters are the writer in human form. Characters, settings, costumes have no existence apart from the writer's words. The words of the script reveal the play and the role each part has in it.

Logos gives us the word and also the concept of logic. One trait of God is logic and from logic comes the subsequent Law of Non-contradiction which states that something cannot both be and not be at the same time and in the same respect. *A* is not *non-A*. Language (both the Word and words) depends on this either/or logic. Without logic's necessary Law of Non-contradiction language could not communicate meaning. If good equals bad and painting equals poem, what would "The poem is good" communicate?

When we read words in a script or hear a word spoken on stage or screen, we assume it comes from the writer or speaker. Something about the words (the penmanship, the tone of voice, etc.) or the circumstances within which the words are uttered (in a subway, at a table in an expensive restaurant) prompts us to imagine the kind of person who could utter the words. As Dorothy Sayers notes, "Quite simply, every choice of an episode, or a phrase, or a word is made to conform to a pattern of the entire [work], which is revealed by that choice as already existing."[48]

We do this because we know the self being expressed through our words. Our words carry us with them. Our words carry our meaning—the thought, feeling, or action you or I hope to convey to whomever receives our words. George Steiner states, "Language, in an overall sense, is a rule-governed system of arbitrarily conventional markers, vocal and graphic, whose function it is to communicate and record significance"(meaning).[49]

Every word comes from an *I*. Every word is a piece of *I's* mind. Through our words we offer others our thoughts and feelings and a share of our life. And since our life has meaning, the words that emanate from us have meaning as well. As the writer Walker Percy said, art "tells the reader how things are, how we are, in a way that the reader can confirm with as much certitude as a scientist taking a pointer-reading."[50]

Through words, one soul impacts another soul. As mere marks or sounds, words are nothing. But as projections of our mentality, our soul, they hook into our minds and spirits, and in the process gain their power. If we do not know Spanish or Greek, we just hear sounds or see lines on paper; they have no emotional or intellectual influence on us because they have no meaning for us. They are like the moos of a cow, the peckings of a chicken.

If our experiences are the material for our story, then words are the forms we use to shape them. Dorothy Sayers points out that language "is an expression of experience and of the relation of one experience to the other. Further, its meaning is realized only in experience. We frequently say, 'Until I had that experience, I never knew what the word fear (or love, or anger, or whatever it is) meant. The language, which had been merely pictorial, is transmitted into experience and we then have immediate knowledge of the reality behind the picture.'"[51]

The power and meaning of words depend on the personality the words convey. When you know what meaning the words carry, the power is immediate. If you hear the word *kitten*, and know the meaning of the word, you respond immediately. You do not need to first ask, "How shall I think of these sounds making *kitten*?" As one speaks and as you hear, the general meaning, the categorical object concerning us instantly comes into existence in your mind. But it is only an analogy: "The fact is, that all language about everything is analogical; we think in a series of metaphors. We can explain nothing in terms of itself, but only in terms of other things."[52]

When we write or speak words, we send meaning. If there are multiple meanings for words, they may exist in our imaginations, but not in the words sent. Our words contain our meaning. You and I are the authority of our meaning and of our words. George Steiner says, "Language is its own past. The meanings of a word are its history, recorded and unrecorded. They are its usage. Prior usage does not, or only very exceptionally, attach to any color or musical sound a specificity of meaning. Words mean. In the most rigorous sense, meaning is etymology. Each word comes to us, as we learn and use a language, with a more or less measureless freight of precedent. It will, where it pertains to common speech, have been thought, spoken, written million fold. This priority and circulation determines, over-determines its meaning and meanings."[53]

When we read or hear words—from a script, a play, or a film—we could be interested in what is meant. The author or speaker appreciates that, because that is why those words were selected and uttered. His words may mean something different to us. If so, we should take that into account when writing or speaking about his words.

But if we read or hear words intended for another, or if the words aren't tailored specifically to our circumstances, then either we can choose to assume the meaning we have for the words (and be in error), or we can try to learn what the words meant to the author or speaker. That would respect the author or speaker because we cared to understand what was shared with us. Or we could ignore whatever meaning the writer or speaker hoped to send, and give the words our meaning. That would disrespect the speaker or author. We would care more about our meaning, than about his meaning—more about us than about him.

Is it possible to ever know another as well as we know ourselves? No. Is it, then, ever possible to know the part of one represented by the words of the script, the play or the film, as well as the author or speaker knows himself? Again, no. But some people know scripts, plays, and films, better than others, and some understand other people better than others. We need to care to know others and their words as well as we can. We all need to be understood.

Are all attempts to know others and their words ultimately doomed to failure? If we define success as knowing others as well as we know ourselves, then yes, we are doomed. But if we define success as knowing others as well as we are able, then we can certainly succeed. As Chesterton notes, "The artist is a person who communicates something...but it is a question of communication and not merely of what some people call expression. Or rather, strictly speaking, unless it is communication it is not expression....the artist does ultimately exhibit himself as being intelligent by being intelligible. I do not say by being easy to understand, but certainly by being understood."[54]

In trying to know others' words, we bring to the task various preconceptions, biases, and limitations, and these impact our work. But the more we try to overcome these things, or set them aside, the better we will get to know the words, scripts, plays, and films. We try to be as objective and sure as possible, knowing that total objectivity and absolute certainty are not possible for any of us. Our knowledge of other people and their words is always provisional. We always keep in mind that the meaning they tried to share with us is not infinite in kind. They had something specific in mind. They hope we care to know what it is. We use our imagination and sensitivities to discover it, not to invent it.

To understand the words of a script, we first seek the ordinary meaning of the language. We identify the literary style of the language, and then seek the single meaning intended by the author. We also need to understand the historical, physical, and cultural frames within which the language exists. These frames include the personal situation of the author and any historical, geographical, or biological references in the script. We use extra-textual sources, such as dictionaries, encyclopedias, handbooks, histories, and commentaries.

Our process is known as *exegesis,* getting out of the words the meaning that is there, no more and no less. We make sure to avoid *eisogesis*, reading into a text something that isn't there at all. Creativity in the dramatic theater is not creativity in reading—finding alternative logics, senses, or implications; undermining the clarity and authority of the scriptwriter; discovering meanings not intended.

The poet Donald Hall wrote, "Words seem like drops of water in a stream that has its own wholeness and its own motion. But when you write well, each word is accurate and honest and exact in itself and contributes its special history to the wholeness of the stream of meaning."[55] "We seek to become sensitive to the words of a script by taking them as literally as possible. By doing so, we are able to respond to the images, pictures, and metaphors in the words. The picture—which we receive by literal reading—gives us the emotion, without losing the idea…that the picture expresses."[56]

The words of the script conjure the images and pictures which will eventually appear on the stage or on the screen. Donald Hall continues: "Images are groups of words that give an impression to the senses. Most images are visual, but we can also make images of taste, touch, hearing, and smell. Images communicate feeling, and locate them firmly, really talking from writer to reader."[57]

Every form must have content and every story is made of words. Words seek to communicate personal, individual experiences that are significant, which have meaning. Story is God's chosen form to elevate our personal experiences toward His universal truth. As writer and actor Nigel Forde wrote, "We must continue to tell our stories, to explore our experience of those vast abstracts such as love and death and misery and sacrifice and forgiveness and redemption in concrete fictions that can shake the mind and the heart. For, in the end, there is nothing else worth talking about. Man's relationship to the universe and to his God, the actual compared to the ideal, is the stuff of all comedy and all tragedy, and the Christian voice should echo through literature, through the nation's memory, as loudly as any other."[58]

CHAPTER 3

The Material Cause of the Dramatic Theater

The Natural Materials Used to Make the Dramatic Theater

Everything that is was created out of nothing by God.

The theater artist's creation, on the other hand, is made from existing materials. Aristotle claimed the basic material of dramatic characters is the same as the basic material of life—suffering or undergoing. So, as in life, the materials of plays and films are human beings in action—seeking and finding, losing and winning, rising and falling, coming and going, suffering, deciding, and discovering to death or to a new life. King Solomon reflected on the cyclical nature of human actions—giving birth and dying; planting and uprooting; killing and healing; tearing down and building up; weeping and laughing; mourning and dancing; throwing stones and gathering stones; embracing and shunning; searching and giving up as lost; keeping and throwing away; tearing apart and sewing together; being silent and speaking; loving and hating; warring and making peace.[1]

Though bronze, Moses' fiery serpent was recognized as a serpent. Bronze was special, chosen rather than snake tissue because the metal could endure and draw people to the light it reflected. The materials of the dramatic theater are human experiences and understandings—of the world, of others, of oneself and of God. Our experiences and understanding may be individual, familial, cultural, or universal. The artist takes his experience and understanding and imagines it in words and pictures. Donald Hall wrote, "Imagination depends upon experience, upon understanding ourselves and the people we have known. The story maker creates a world of strangers based upon a lifetime of friends and acquaintances."[2] Director George Cukor said, "everything influences you–you walk down the street, you look at this, you read a book–everything."[3]

The play *Hamlet* comes from William Shakespeare's experiences and understanding. Born and

raised in Stratford, England, a rural farming town
of 1,500 souls, to Catholic Christian parents, the
young man was educated in his faith and in his local
grammar school. Though small, the town boasted
of the beautiful thirteenth century Church of the
Holy Trinity and an even older chapel of the Guild
of the Holy Cross. As the village schoolteacher, he
may have come across a Norse legend composed by
Saxo Grammaticus in Latin around 1200 AD called
Hamlet. But Saxo's text did not appear in English
until 1608, so either Shakespeare was fluent in
French or he used another English source based on
the French translation. Critic Stephen Greenblatt at-
tributes Shakespeare's success, in part, to his ability
to recall and use his personal experiences.

Whether or not he had access to the Hamlet
play, Shakespeare had to an astounding degree
something that virtually every actor at the time
had to possess: an acute memory. Everything he
encountered, even tangentially and in passing,
seems to have stayed with him and remained
available to him years later. Scraps of conversation, official proclamations, long-winded
sermons, remarks overheard in the tavern or
on the street, insults exchanged by carters and
fishwives, a few pages that he could only have
glanced at idly in a bookseller's shop—all was
somehow stored away in his brain, in files that his

imagination could open up at will. His memory was not perfect — he made mistakes, confused one place for another, transposed names, and the like—but the imperfections only demonstrate that there was nothing compulsive or mechanical about his remarkable gift. His memory was an immense creative resource.[4]

Probably the young actor came across the earlier play based on this Norse legend by Thomas Kyd, called the *Ur-Hamlet* performed on the London stage. Shakespeare had recently returned to his hometown to bury his only son, Hamnet, and shortly, his father John. Around the time of these funerals Shakespeare began to write his own version of the popular play focusing on death's destruction of the universal father and son relationship. As C. S. Lewis notes, "I believe that we read Hamlet's speeches with interest chiefly because they describe so well a certain spiritual region through which most of us have passed and anyone in his circumstances might be expected to pass, rather than because of our concern to understand how and why this particular man entered it."[5]

Faced with his own father's and son's deaths, Shakespeare clearly shared Hamlet's sense of horror that his beloveds' "canonised bones, hearséd in death / Have burst their cerements." Shakespeare's childhood Catholic education ran deep. Many passages echo the English translation of Saint Carlo Borromeo's *Last Will of the Soul* found hidden in the roof of his father's house. The testament sought to help the Christian resist Satan's temptations at the hour of death. The words echo in those of the ghost of Hamlet's father:

Cut off even in the blossoms of my sin,
Unhous'led, disappointed, unanel'd,
No reck'ning made, but sent to my account
With all my imperfections on my head.
O, horrible, O, horrible, most horrible!

The artist must have been so appalled by those who met their maker "unaneled" that he has Hamlet spare his father's murderer: "No!" he cries,

Up sword, and know thou a more horrid hent:
When he is...
...about some act
That has no relish of salvation in't...
...that his soul may be as damn'd and black
As hell, whereto it goes.

The ghost of Hamlet's father, a role played by Shakespeare himself, lives in purgatory:

My hour is almost come
When I to sulph'rous and tormenting flames

Must render up myself...
Doomed for a certain term to walk the night,
And for the day confined to fast in fires,
Till the foul crimes done in my days of nature
Are burnt and purged away.

While Kyd's Ophelia dies by falling over a cliff's edge, Shakespeare's heroine drowns amid a profusion of Warwickshire flowers:

Crowflowers, nettles, daisies, and long purples
That liberal shepherds give a grosser name,
But our cold maids do deadmen's fingers call them.

The scriptwriter is recalling the girl, Kate Hamnet, who drowned herself, possibly for love, a mile from Stratford when Shakespeare was a boy. The kingdom of God broke through into William Shakespeare's life, forcing him to confront his mortality. The result was *Hamlet*.

As with Shakespeare, the life experiences and understanding of screenwriter Budd Schulberg and director Elia Kazan shaped their imagining of *On the Waterfront*. In January 1952, Kazan was called before the House Committee on Un-American Activities (HUAC). In the early 1930s he had been a founding member of the leftist Group Theater in New York. And for a year and a half, beginning in 1934, he was a member of the Communist Party. Kazan admitted that he had been a member of the party while with the Group Theater. He quit the party, he claimed "in disgust." A committed liberal, Kazan felt betrayed by the atrocities of Stalin and the ideological rigidity of the Stalinists. He was personally offended when party functionaries tried to intervene in the artistic decisions of his theater group.

He denied the accusation that the Group Theater was a "front" organization, and that its three directors were Communists. But among the names Kazan gave the committee were the great writer Clifford Odets (who himself would later "name names"), Lee and Paula Strasburg, Lillian Hellman, Joe Bromberg, and John Garfield.

After his testimony, his fellow stage and film co-workers maligned Kazan. But Kazan's best defense was his 1954 film portraying a young hood who becomes disillusioned—after experiencing an invasion of the kingdom of God—with the gangsters who control the local longshoreman's union. The rule on the docks, enforced by terror, was that union members were supposed to be "deaf and dumb"—to pretend they didn't know anything about the gang and to refuse to speak to the police. The hero of the film is the one man who has the courage to break this code of silence and testify against the gang. "Terry Malloy felt as I did. He felt ashamed and proud of himself at the same time. He wavered between the two, and he also felt hurt by the fact that people—his own friends—were rejecting him. He also felt that it was a necessary act. He felt like a fool, but proud of himself because he found out that he was better than the other people around him."[6]

Kazan had the hero speak for him:

When Brando, at the end, yells at Lee Cobb, the mob boss, "I'm glad what I done–you hear me?–glad what I done!" that was me saying, with identical heat, that I was glad that I'd testified as I had. I'd been snubbed by friends each and every day for many months in my old show business haunts, and I'd not forgotten nor would I forgive the men, old friends some of them, who'd snubbed me, so the scene in the film where Brando goes back to the waterfront to "shape up" again for employment and is rejected by men with whom he'd worked day after day—that, too, was my story, now told to all the world. So when critics say that I put my story and my feelings on the screen, to justify my informing, they are right. That transference of emotion from my own experience to the screen is the merit of those scenes.[7]

Kazan intended the film as a metaphor for his decision to testify against his former comrades in the party. Schulberg based his screenplay on his novel *Waterfront*, a result of his one-year investigation of the waterfront, its neighbors, the Manhattan Bowers Mob, and the Hoboken, New Jersey and Red Hook, Brooklyn piers. He became involved with the crusading Jesuit priest, Father John Corridan ("Father Pete"), co-director of St. Francis Xavier Labor School, founded in 1936 to fight communism by promoting Christian principles.

As the story developed, Terry Malloy became an informer on the illegal activities that Schulberg discovered. Kazan said,

> The script was based on a set of real events...It was based on the life of a guy named DiVincenzo, who I knew, whose house I ate at."[8] "I knew the waterfront in Hoboken intimately. I spent months there. Schulberg spent a month there."[9] "I was in touch with the guys whose lives were being threatened at that moment. There were gangsters watching me shoot the picture...This wasn't fiction. I was dealing with people's lives. I knew the children who were not getting enough to eat because thugs were taking kickbacks out of their fathers' pay. It was great because they were loading and unloading boats while we were shooting pictures on the same pier. I was photographing life. The issues we were dramatizing were happening right there, all around us."[10]

Budd Schulberg, on the other hand, denied the film was influenced by his testimony to the House committee. He did say, however that "snitch may be a dirty word, but standing up for the truth, paying the price of the whistle blower, is the other side of that coin."[11]

Artists of the dramatic theater, like William Shakespeare, Budd Schulberg, and Elia Kazan, transform their personal, familial, cultural, and universal, but fleeting, experiences with the kingdom of God through their fiery imaginations into special words and pictures, which endure, like bronze, to resonate as true, good, and beautiful in lands and times far from those of the artists. Universal appreciation begins in a personal encounter. Director Leo McCarey tells of the personal story that served as the basis for his film *Going My Way*:

> [T]here was an eccentric little old priest who was the head of the parish at Santa Monica [from December 1923 to his death in March 1949], Monsignor Conneally. There were a million stories about him, his eccentricities. In fact, he became so famous, his name was a legend. One day he came to our house looking for a handout for the church; he gave me quite a long speech about opening my heart and my purse strings, et cetera. I said, "OK, Father—while I'm in the mood, let me go—I have nothing but holly in my heart."

"OK, my lad," he said. So I go in the house to write out the check. I wrote what I thought was a big check, for twenty-five hundred dollars, and gave it to him. He glanced at it, folded it up and put it into his pocket; he didn't say anything, and he started away. I said, "Just a minute, father. Did you notice the amount of that check?" And he said, "Yes, I did"; then he said, "Well, maybe next Sunday you would like for me to thank you from the pulpit and tell the congregation how much money you gave?" I didn't want him to do that and I told him so; I said, "You're a hard man to do business with—I feel ashamed of myself." And the old man said, "You should. Pat O'Brien just gave me five thousand." With that, he was gone.[12]

As the traits of God are known through what God does, so the traits of human beings and dramatic characters are known by what they do. The personal experiences of William Shakespeare, Budd Schulberg, Elia Kazan, and Leo McCarey reveal characters with certain typical behaviors. Behaviors may be biological, physical, dispositional, social, deliberative, or ethical. Some behaviors are common to all members of our species; these are *universal* behaviors. Other behaviors identify a distinct *culture*, or society of a particular time and place. Still others are peculiar to an individual *family*. Finally, some behaviors are peculiar to a single person; these are *individual* behaviors. Usually the universal emerges through the individual. As Elia Kazan noted, "We were just trying to make an absolutely characteristic, typical story about that area, that mood and that time. I suppose we were dealing with universals, but I wasn't aware of it."[13]

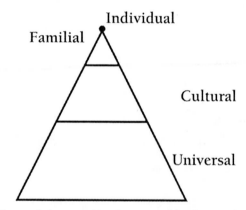

(The one below provides the material for the one above; the one above gives form to the one below.)

In the mid-1960s, anthropologist Laura Bohannan narrated the story of Shakespeare's *Hamlet* to the remote Tiv tribe of West Africa. The tribe had no knowledge of Western theater, drama, and little, if any, notions of Western society. Nevertheless, Ms. Bohannan found the actions of the play familiar and understandable to the tribal audience. In fact, the tribe was able to predict accurately the consequences of certain choices and actions taken by the characters. Occasionally the tribe reconfigured an incident—the ghost was considered an omen sent by a witch, the madness of Hamlet and Ophelia was believed to be caused, like all madness, by witchcraft. In fact, the tribe's understanding of human behavior and motivation filled in the actions Shakespeare presented, adding a novel, yet rich, understanding of the play. (For example, by marrying his brother's widow, Claudius fulfilled Tiv expectations.) Nevertheless, Polonius' words and actions were still foolish to fresh West African hearers. The Tiv even suggested a "responsible" course of action for Hamlet: rather than take revenge, a son should restrain his hand against his uncle by taking his cause to a council of elders.

What allowed people of so different a time and place to understand so much of Shakespeare's world?

In the mid-1970s, British theater director Peter Brook assembled an international company of actors to conduct research into fundamental physical and vocal theatre vocabulary—Le Centre International de Recherche Theatrale (CIRT). The group performed long epics and short playlets before audiences from Iran to Africa, who had never seen a theatrical performance of any kind. The playlets delighted these audiences of the most diverse cultural backgrounds.

What allowed people of so different cultures and places to understand these plays?

In 1983, decades of self-imposed cultural isolation ended when Arthur Miller's drama, *Death of a Salesman*, opened in Beijing, China. The Communist audience cheered the capitalist drama of 1940 American family life.

What allowed people of so different a time and place to understand this play?

What allows people of all times and places to recognize a first century Hebrew rabbi as their friend and redeemer?

Universal Behaviors

Evolutionary biology, evolutionary psychology, and human ethology—the biology of human behavior—have identified species-specific behaviors and behavior patterns, sometimes called *universals*. Universals are genetically programmed cross-cultural behavior patterns characteristic of Homo sapiens.

God has imprinted on the human heart commonalities among us. Theologians and ethicists call this natural law. In human behavior, these are universal behaviors. Movies and plays, which resonate across time and space, may be "special." But as Ellen Dissanayake writes "to make something special generally implies taking care and doing one's best so as to produce a result that is—to a greater or lesser extent—accessible, striking, resonant, and satisfying to those who take the time to appreciate it."[14]

All of us have certain things in common, besides suffering. Human ethologists—biologists who study human behavior—call these things "programs inherent to our cognitive apparatus,"[15] They explain: "Humans possess an innate repertoire of signals as phylogenetic adaptations, and seem capable of understanding a number of these signals prior to individual experience on the basis of innate releasing mechanisms. Due to these biological programs, we are able to communicate across cultural and linguistic barriers."[16]

The common features of our lives—what we all undergo as members of the same species—are necessary to make dramatic theater interesting, important, and universal. In other words, great. Great works of the stage and screen engage and reveal the dynamic relationship among the behaviors of all four types, from individual person through species. Dramatic theatre artists select and order these innate universal behaviors, and mix them with unique cultural, familial, and individual behaviors. Universal behaviors are characteristic of humans in all times and in all places. Ellen Dissanayake observes, "Art's distinctness resides not entirely in its disinterested stratospheric isolation but in its primordial biological rootedness."[17] The extent of our universal "biological rootedness" is impressive.[18]

Suffering

Although humans and all dramatic characters share the common universal of suffering, Christians have an additional meaning when suffering is understood. For the Christian, suffering and rejection are the fruit of discipleship to Jesus Christ. The first suffering is the abandonment of attachment to the things of this world; the first step is death of the old life, and the start of a new life. The next suffering is the bearing of another's burdens and the suffering that forgiveness requires.

Paradoxically, Christian suffering is not tragic, but joyous; not a defeat by suffering, but a victory over suffering through suffering. Director Kazan noted the role of suffering in the change in a dramatic character: "I do believe that events cause people to change, that heroes are made by events as much as events by heroes, and that in difficulty a person gets stronger, harder and more resolute."[19]

John Paul II elaborates: "In so far as it seeks the beautiful fruit of an imagination which rises above the everyday, art is by its nature a kind of appeal to the mystery. Even when they explore the darkest depths of the soul or the most unsettling aspects of

evil, artists give voice in a way to the universal desire
for redemption."[20] Director Mel Gibson found his
personal suffering to be the catalyst to making *The
Passion of the Christ*; the film "had its genesis during
a time in which [he] found [him]self trapped with
feelings of terrible, isolated emptiness."[21]

Actors and writers often speak of the *arc* of the
character. The arc seeks to locate the nature of the
character's change. Change is the essence of drama.
Director Kazan noted, "I put a great stress on the
idea that in a good film or play the protagonist
changes. He's not the same at the end as he is at the
beginning."[22] But God, Christ, and the Holy Spirit
are immutable; they do not change. Consequently,
depending on how they react to an invasion by the
kingdom of God into their lives, characters may be
seen becoming more like Christ or less like Christ.
Nevertheless, in each case, human behavior is the
material; as director George Cukor observed, "human behavior, the human heart, is to me what is
very dramatic and rather complicated; and, I think,
interests and moves the audience."[23]

As with natural law, God places in every heart
the traits necessary to both suffer as Christ, and
experience a breakthrough by the kingdom of God,
whether one is a Christian or not. Consequently, we
can see good, true, and beautiful actions undertaken
by people and dramatic characters of all times and

places. These actions are of God, whether or not the person or character realizes it, because He is goodness, truth and beauty. People and characters that act upon, or evidence, these God-given virtues draw us to them like the fiery serpent. Hamlet and Terry Malloy are prime examples.

The behavior displayed in films and plays acknowledge certain universal, natural dispositions and patterns. For example, in both play and film, characters form closed groups, construct rank orders, maintain territory, and deprecate other groups. For example, the Poles, Norwegians, and Danes, as well as the waterfront union, are all close-knit groups, seeking to defend and expand their territory. Johnny Friendly sits atop the union hierarchy, flanked by his right-hand man, Charlie the Gent. In Poland, Norway and Denmark, kings top the hierarchies, supported chiefly by their oldest sons. Each nation deprecates and fears members of the other. The corrupt union deprecates and fears the members of both the Waterfront Crime Commission and the Catholic Church.

In both *Hamlet* and *On the Waterfront,* the same emotions are evident among the characters. Certain emotions are universal, both in type and manner of expression. Charles Darwin was one of the first investigators to notice that certain expressive movements indicate emotional states for joy, fear, rage, surprise, anguish, interest, shame, contempt, and disgust. The significance of these certain universal innate behaviors is learned culturally. "Emotions are subjective categories, but a self-examination of one's emotions shows that they are accompanied by specific expressive movements (muscle actions). We can even record physiological reactions typical for individual emotions,...and if we compare the statements from members of different cultures we find that there is considerable conformity."[24] "The expressive movements associated with the various emotions are essentially identical in all cultures."[25] The culture of eleventh century Denmark as seen through the eyes of sixteenth century England as well as the culture of 1950s Hoboken each modify the way the same emotions are expressed by accentuating certain features, repressing others, or adding new elements.

In both play and film, kin groups arrange people. Often kin groups come to embody the two competing kingdoms or ages. In *Hamlet*, the sons of the ruling families seek revenge for the deaths of their fathers, as Laertes seeks revenge for the murder of his father, Polonius. In *On the Waterfront*, the hero Terry Malloy is torn between loyalty to his brother Charlie, tied to the corrupt union, and to his girlfriend Edie, whose brother was murdered with Terry's unconscious assistance. And regardless of the kin-group or cultural arrangement, each group in both *Hamlet* and *On the Waterfront* employs universal visual signaling of group identity and rank position through clothing, body decoration, and behavior. Likewise, the groups in each work of dramatic theater employ strategies for group maintenance and bonding. Each group possesses birth, puberty, marriage, and death rites, ritual greetings and farewells. Both worlds of *Hamlet* and *On the Waterfront* have occasions of celebration–the wedding party in *On the Waterfront*—and of mourning—Ophelia's funeral in *Hamlet*. Each world differentiates according to status, divides labor, and values coordination and cooperation in labor.

In both play and film, audiences see the organization of communities based on natural law, kingdom principles. In both worlds murder is considered wrong and subject to justice. In both worlds loyalty is valued, and familial and erotic love is encouraged. Individual submission to the authority of the state, the group, the parent, or the husband is seen as natural. Conflict arises as each hero chooses between conflicting loyalties and demands on his obedience.

Both worlds reveal characters using tools (guns, swords, and daggers), trading and exchanging goods or services (money), eating cooked foods, giving gifts, joking, calling one another by personal names, playing, dancing, singing, making music, adorning bodies, using calendars as a coherent perception of time and space, counting, and using language to communicate meaning. Terry's changing from his plaid jacket, to a suit, to the murdered Joey's windbreaker visualizes his arc of development, just as Hamlet's change of hand tool from skull to sword reflects his inner psychological arc.

In both *Hamlet* and *On the Waterfront,* language is used creatively. Instances of lying and deception occur. Characters use metaphors. Hamlet feigns madness as part of his strategy, while Terry Malloy both deceives and is deceived by his union and family. Terry eventually decides to use the truth as his primary weapon.

Our universal employment of strategies of fighting and conflict, display and bluffing, challenging, attacking, defending, withdrawing, reconciling and peace making are evident in films and plays. In each work, audiences form—in *Hamlet*, to watch the climactic mousetrap play; in *On the Waterfront*, to watch the climactic Waterfront Crime Commission hearings. In each dramatic work, the main characters tell stories to one another. Hamlet relates his escape from the death plot at sea, and Terry Malloy tells his brother of his chance to "be a contender" and tells Edie his life story in a bar.

Deliberative and ethical universals—glimpses of kingdom rule—govern the worlds of *Hamlet* and *On the Waterfront.* A transcendent power that is worshiped is acknowledged in each world; a priest in *Hamlet* officiates at Ophelia's funeral, while Father Barry gives the last rites to "Kayo" Dugan. As St. Thomas Aquinas notes, "All the civilizations of mankind that have ever existed were rooted in religion and a quest for God"[26] Ivar Lissner adds, "Human beings are spiritual animals. Indeed, there is a case for arguing that *Homo sapiens* are also *homo religious.*"[27]

In plays and films, everyone worships something. Characters, like people, need something on which to focus their lives. For some, it is work; for others, pleasure. Power, fame, love, knowledge, money, sex, drugs, nation, physical beauty or prowess, family, friends, and humanity itself have all been aspects of the kingdom of this world on which men and women have focused their lives and worship, rather than on the kingdom of God.

Sexual restrictions to behavior apply in both *Hamlet* and *On the Waterfront*. Hamlet tells Ophelia to get to a "nunnery"; Terry tells Edie that pigeons are faithful to one mate. Both dramatic worlds feature the institution of a court and the ideas of good and bad, true and false, beautiful and ugly. St. Thomas Aquinas observed, "The light of natural reason, whereby we discern what is good and what is evil, which is the function of the natural law, is nothing else than an imprint on us of the divine light"[28]

Neither world makes murder a virtue or gratitude a vice, thereby evidencing a natural law based on kingdom principles constructed out of universally known objective moral principles.

Natural law—kingdom authority—is imprinted by God in our brain, directing both us and the dramatic characters toward our natural good. The worlds of film and plays forbid incest, have legal codes and penal sanctions based on natural law. Karen Armstrong notes, "Now all men know the truth to a certain extent, at least as to the common principles of the natural law."[29] Both worlds also have procedures governing inheritance.

In both *Hamlet* and *On the Waterfront*, passionate characters—primarily Claudius and Johnny Friendly—are seen trying to overturn certain natural laws. Such attempts resemble cultural constructions (like the Egyptian monarchy's insistence on incestuous marriage, or the modern denial of God's existence) and are viewed as distortions of nature. Characters sometimes seek individual exceptions or seek justification through individual or group persuasion. Claudius, Terry Malloy, and his brother Charlie try to justify behavior that violates the natural law.

Outside kingdom rule, when natural law is overthrown, ethics become merely the ability to impose one's will on another—Claudius seeks to impose his will on Denmark and Johnny Friendly seeks to impose his will on the waterfront. Without universal reference points in Claudius' court or Johnny Friendly's union hall, rational discussion, persuasion, and consensus among the characters become pointless and absurd. All that remains is the sheer exercise of power.

Cultural Behaviors

Some thinkers have denied the existence of universal behaviors. They believe all behaviors are the constructions of cultures. However, *cultural behaviors* are properly understood as the manifestation of the universal, adapted to a particular time and place. The significance or meaning of the innate universal is learned culturally. The way the universals of a particular time and place manifest themselves is known as a particular culture. For example, a particular religion —the Greek pantheon for example—is the cultural manifestation of the spiritual impulse of a specific time and place—Greece, fifth century BC. Our species naturally believes in God, the transcendent power; particular cultures teach the details of their understanding of God, or their disbelief in God. Culture creates certain behaviors, including denial, surrounding its understanding of God.

The culture of *Hamlet* manifests the universals in ways distinct from *On the Waterfront*. Though both worlds speak English, dialects are in evidence as well as slang and jargon. Though music, fighting, and decoration are common to each world, the particular kinds are distinct while serving the same human functions. Work is common in both worlds, even though the type of work is distinct to each culture.

Family Behaviors

A family, whether in the royal court of Denmark or in the streets of Hoboken, New Jersey, is a group of people sharing a common ancestry. *Hamlet* is a play about families in conflict—the Hamlet family, the Fortinbras family, and the Polonius family. *On the Waterfront* features two broken families—the Malloy family and the Doyle family—and one group opposing their unity—the Johnny Friendly mob—and one group advocating their unity—the Catholic Church of Father Barry. The family is the smallest cultural unit. In a family, for example, a particular religion—Catholicism—may be that specific family's manifestation of the spiritual impulse.

Family is a biological, procreative, and child-rearing structure. In both dramatic works, some families are destroyed while others grow. Through hereditary and environmental influences, a family typically shares goals and values, long-term commitments, a household, a common culture, and economic and other resources for socialization.

A culture's biological and marital kinship rules and patterns of reciprocal obligations define family. Each culture defines who is biological and marital kin, and who is not kin, and the obligations kin have to one another. In one culture, kinship may be based on the father's biological line; in another, kinship may be based on the mother's biological line; in another, kinship is based on a combination of both the father and mother's biological lines. The rules for kinship and marital family relationships are virtually unlimited. Different rules apply for *Hamlet* than for *On the Waterfront*.

While the members of a family see their identity as importantly attached to the group's identity, an individual person's sense of attachment or estrangement is important in defining a family. Hamlet feels estranged from the beginning of the play. Terry grows estranged as he learns the truth of both his brother and surrogate family, the union of Johnny Friendly. Thus, abused or estranged biological offspring may sever their psychological associations with the family and effectively dissolve the family. Others, who are not biological kin, may consider themselves to be "family" and effectively create or join an existing family.

Individual Behaviors

Some thinkers have even denied the existence of individual personhood. The unique particularization of the species' universals, a culture's distinct channeling of common impulses, and a family's mores in which certain impulses and educations are more prominent than others characterize the individual. Individual behaviors are a function of personality and personhood. Personhood is not personality.

Personality is a collection of properties formed by genetics and environment. Beyond the genetics of the environmentally conditioned physical body, a human being is a spirit or soul.[30] The soul contains one's intellect, emotions, and will. Human beings are created to have a unity between the body and soul; every human action involves both and is the whole person acting. The soul is the immaterial part of a person that lives on after death. A soul contains the mind's sensations, thoughts, beliefs, desires, and acts of will.[31]

Personhood involves those aspects of the body and soul created by God. A human being is a soul; a human being has a body. Personality develops gradually in the course of a lifetime; personhood arrives instantly at conception. Even as a zygote, a human soul has the body needed to function as a self-integrated human being. During our brief time on earth, God has given us time and space to make decisions, to shape our lives, to respond to His Word, and to seek or reject His kingdom rule. If we respond affirmatively to His offer, and make His son the Lord of our lives, we become new creatures through the symbolic death and resurrection of baptism. The process has been compared to that of a flashlight. Until the batteries are accepted and installed, there is a void seeking fulfillment. When the batteries are accepted, and the switch is flipped, the flashlight has its new existence and function as a light in the world.

When the human body dies, the time for deciding has past. The burden of our human freedom is lifted as our testing pilgrimage ends. As a result of our lifetime examination, our soul continues to live by virtue of the powers that belong to its nature—consciousness, imagination, reason, and desire—as it leaves the body. The soul then either continues in, or apart from, the presence of the living God forever.

The scientist John Polkinghorne has elaborated on what being an individual soul means: "a self-conscious being, able to use the future tense in anticipation, hope, and dread; able to perceive meaning and to assign value; able to respond to beauty and to the call of moral duty; able to love other persons, even to the point of self-sacrifice. To this I would also wish to add an explicit religious dimension arising from the sense of a reality beyond oneself, without whose gracious sustaining power life is incomplete, a reality which is the ground of value and being and to whom the proper response its worship and obedience."[32]

The individual—whether Hamlet or Terry Malloy—gives each play or film its unique point of view. Though similar in many important universal, cultural, and even familial ways, both Hamlet and Terry Malloy are distinct individual characters. The maker of a play or film chooses what parts of a story to emphasize in the plot. Later the director, actors, and designers bring their various points of view to the work. In viewing, we the audience, despite efforts by the director, actors, and designer to focus our attention, can choose which part of the stage picture to attend and which to ignore. With film, we see only as the filmmaker wants us to see. Donald Hall calls this point of view, "either your own, viewing all of your characters' minds as if you were God; or one of your characters, a 'he' or an 'I', whose mind you read. Point of view helps unity and focus."[33]

As a point of view is applied to individual experiences, the material begins to take a shape, a form. Brian Godawa says that form is a story following "a main character who seeks a specific goal and in so doing learns something about himself or herself and the world in a way that inevitably results in this person's redemption—or lack thereof."[34] Both Hamlet and Terry Malloy confront a breakthrough from the kingdom of God, and in the process, learn about themselves in ways that lead to their transformation.

CHAPTER 4

The Efficient Cause of the Dramatic Theater

The Power that Causes a Work of Dramatic Theater to Come into Being Its Relationship to the Power that Causes Creation

The planarian is a microscopic kind of flat-worm with a simple central nervous system. Every planarian exhibits what is known as *phototactic behavior*—in other words, it tends to position its body toward the light. It is a universal characteristic of the species. What is the power which causes this behavior? Were planarians taught to turn to the light? No, even a planarian isolated from birth will repeat the same behavior. Do planarians orient toward light as an act of free will? Probably not. The odds of every planarian making the same choice are slim. Perhaps genetically inherited instructions compel each planarian within the species to respond to the light in the same way. This seems to be the explanation, since only damaged or abnormal planarians fail to perform this characteristic action.

Would planarians be genetically disposed to turn toward something that didn't exist? No. Planarians are hardwired to turn to light because light exists. Human beings, likewise, turn toward things because they exist. Water is desired because water exists, and it is possible for people to fulfill this desire. Food is desired because food exists, and it is possible for people to fulfill this desire. Sex is desired because sex exists, and it is possible for people to fulfill this desire. Sleep is possible because sleep exists, and it is possible for people to fulfill this desire.

We, like the snake-bitten Israelites, turn to the light, even light reflected by a work of art. Our species seems genetically conceived to turn toward a transcendent being for the power we need. We do so because the light exists and because the light fulfills our need.

Light, best defined as a series of packets of energy, is also a form of energy. When light shines, energy is transmitted. For example, the amount of energy falling on the Earth's surface from the sun is approximately 5.6 quintillion megajoules per year. The energy input from the sun in a single day could supply the needs of all of the Earth's inhabitants for a period of about three decades. Scientists believe that the total amount of energy in the universe is constant—no more can be added and no more can be removed. The only thing that can happen is the transformation of energy into different types of energy—energy to satisfy a planarian, to protect a snake-bitten Israelite, or to transform our experiences into works of dramatic theater.

We have desires because energy exists to fulfill them. Philosophers, theologians, and biologists consider this the argument from desire: every natural desire corresponds to some real state of affairs that can fulfill it. God, the light, is desired because He is the source of all energy and power. He brought all creation—planarians, snakes, and people alike—into being. He is the source of the power needed to transform experience into a story by the artists of the dramatic theater.

Planarians did not create light. Human beings did not invent water, food, sex, sleep, or God. The source of the desires and the power to fulfill those desires transcend time and space. The power which caused the universe and causes life to come into being, is God.

God has all power and all wisdom. Pope John Paul II declared, "O Lord, how many are Your works! In wisdom you have made them all."[1] God is author and scriptwriter, and reality is His story. Dramatic theater is a human story, invaded by the kingdom of God. Aristotle said, "All art is concerned with coming into being, i.e. with contriving and considering how something may come into being which is capable of either being or not being, and whose origin is in the maker and not in the thing made."[2] Dramatic theater shows the birth of a new creation following a breakthrough by the kingdom of God.

The fiery serpent came into being through the power of its maker. All the Israelites fixed their eyes on it. Likewise, all human beings fix their eyes on God, the power and efficient cause of creation. For example, in Athens, Epimenides named Him the unknown God. Xenophanes, Plato, and Aristotle used Theos as the personal name for the supreme God. The Incas knew Viracocha, the omnipotent creator of all things. The Santal of India called him Thakur Jiu, the genuine god. The Gedeo of Ethiopia worshipped Magano, the omnipotent creator of all. The African Republic's Mbaka (a Bantu tribe) know Koro, the creator. In China, Shang Ti is the Lord of Heaven. Koreans call Hananim, the Great One. In Burma, the Karen know Y'wa, the Supreme God.

The Mizo of India acknowledge Panthian, the one supreme God.

Every culture has perceived reality as having two power sources—the natural and the supernatural. The Hebrew metallurgist used both powers to shape his bronze serpent; the wise artists of the dramatic theater use both as well. Natural power, temporary, is of the Present Age; supernatural power, eternal, is of the Age to Come. Belief in a universal supernatural realm of power is inherent in the human species. The earliest humans were commonly monotheistic. Wilhelm Schmidt has documented the evidence for native monotheism in *The Origin of the Concept of God* in 1912 (By 1955 he had collected twelve volumes of evidence.) Ivar Lissner notes that "ethnology has established an extremely interesting fact which is all too little appreciated. All the primitive peoples in the world possess a tradition of a supreme god, and all primitive peoples are aware of a divine manifestation."[3] Polytheism and the proliferation of gods arose when cultures and tribes met and blended. Pantheism is the cultural elaboration of this blending. Thomas Aquinas summed it up: "It seems that the existence of God is self-evident. Those things are said to be self-evident to us the knowledge of which is naturally implanted in us."

Humans universally seek power from one God, one eternal, omnipresent, omnipotent, omniscient creator of reality, and the embodiment of supernatural power. As Euripides noted, "If God is truly God, he is perfect, lacking nothing." So universal is the belief in God, that atheism must be taught. Atheism is a social or psychological construction; Paul Vitz concludes, "there is a coherent psychological origin to intense atheism"[4] The philosopher John MacMurray has speculated that the roots of atheism might even lie in a child's urge to parricide: "The wish to destroy the father and take his place is one of the common phantasies of childhood. Would it not be as good an argument as Freud's…if we were to conclude that adult atheism was a projection upon the universe of this phantasy."[5]

Atheism denies supernatural power from a single personal spiritual being who created the world from nothing, who transcends the physical universe and sustains it by His immanent power, who has imprinted universal laws in His creation, who cares for every living thing by His providence, who fashioned us in His own image, who revealed both Himself and His will to us, who metes out eternal rewards and punishments, and whose kingdom invades our lives by His grace. Nevertheless, this grace lets God rain His spiritual power on believers and unbelievers alike: "You send forth the Your Spirit, they are created; And You renew the face of the ground."[6]

The innate desire to know and worship God can, according to Thomas Oden, be "intellectually twisted, morally stunted, and developmentally skewed. It is distortable into polytheisms, idolatries, animisms, superstitions, and pantheisms of various sorts."[7] The denial of God needs support from familial, social, and cultural forces to overcome the genetic disposition to seek the Light. As Elie Weisel stated of the Holocaust, "How strange that the philosophy denying God came not from the survivors. Those who came out with the so-called God-is-dead theology, not one of them had been in Auschwitz. Those who had never said it."[8]

We seek God's power by imitating Him. All people seek to imitate God the Creator's ability to make stories. As Aristotle wrote in chapter four of his *Poetics*, "It is natural for all to delight in works of imitation." The beauty of His natural creation prompts us to copy. In fact, Elaine Scarry notes, "the requirement beauty places on us to replicate, the simplest manifestation of the phenomenon is the everyday fact of staring."[9] The philosopher Ludwig Wittgenstein said that "when the eye sees something beautiful, the hand wants to draw it."[10]

Consequently, the power that causes the dramatic theater to come to life is an aspect of the power of God—wisdom. We imagine fictional human beings in invented circumstances. We organize those imaginings with learned or innate skill sufficient to elicit from our audience the same reactions it would have had to actual people in real life circumstances. Aristotelian scholar Kenneth Telford notes, "An art work can be effected either by means of a learned rational productive faculty which constitutes an art or by means of an habituation which is a part of man's natural abilities undirected by reason."[11] In other words, the theater artist can either learn how to make a story out of his experiences by acquiring the power of knowledge, or he may employ a natural, in-born gift or talent for story making.

Wise teachers and thoughtful books can provide the knowledge of various dramatic arts; the grace of God can provide natural aptitudes or talents for certain dramatic arts. The eternal God replicates himself in His earthly children by sharing his power to make. Created by God's power to live forever in Paradise, fallen humans seek His power of eternal life. He offers it in the kingdom of God, Already Here but Not Yet.

Many dramatic theater artists seek the immortality of God on the stage and screen. They want to survive as the fittest, but come up with stories that media critics call violent. They want to reproduce, but produce what media critics call sex. George Steiner notes that "the successful dramatist or story-teller or painter is 'God' in large miniature. He or she ushers into the world agents out of the imaginary, out of some dust of pre-existence, whose subsequent fate, whose freedom of action can, precisely as in the mystery of free will accorded by God to His creations, challenge the maker."[12]

Many plays and films reproduce aspects of the artists' own lives. Chesterton says, "Lost somewhere in the enormous plains of time, there wanders a dwarf who is the image of God, who has produced on a yet more dwarfish scale, an image of creation. The pigmy picture of God we call Man; the pigmy picture of creation we call Art. It is an undervaluing of the function of man to say that he only expresses his own personality....His business (as something secondary but divine) is to make the world over again, and that is the meaning of all portraits and public buildings"[13]

Budd Schulberg, the screenwriter of *On the Waterfront*, was raised in a household filled with wisdom about the art of screenwriting. His father, Ben, wrote for one of the earliest film journals, *Film Reports*. Vachel Lindsay's *The Art of the Moving Pictures* gave the elder Schulberg a strong connection between social activism and screenwriting. As Schulberg wrote, "I came into the world hearing not the strains of 'Rock-a-Bye, Baby" or 'Just a Song at Twilight', but the clicking of typewriter keys."[14] Some of that typing was composing the preface to

A.W. Thomas's *How to Write a Photoplay*. The Schulberg family was wise in the art of the dramatic theater: "If we had no family tree, yet ours was another kind of family, stretching horizontally, composed of motion-picture pioneers with whom my father the writer soon found himself involved."[15]

Like his son, Schulberg's father was an avid boxing fan. In fact, Ben Schulberg uttered the most famous line in his son's film, *On the Waterfront* —"He coulda been a contenda"–in reference to a fighter named Benny Leonard.[16]

But there is no direct correspondence between the knowledge of how to make a work of dramatic theater and the ability to actually make one. Some scholars deny that William Shakespeare wrote the plays attributed to him because his brief education could not possibly produce plays of that quality. On the other hand, many artists with natural ability never create the body of works the world hoped they would. Even more telling, history points to men with little knowledge and no discernable natural gifts who created important films and plays. How does that happen?

There is a story of a young, talented actor engaged to perform at the retirement dinner of a beloved pastor. The actor had prepared the pastor's favorite text, the twenty-third Psalm. After dinner, the actor rose and presented the text to considerable applause. More tributes followed until the retiring pastor himself stood to acknowledge the tributes. In the course of his remarks, the pastor began to recite Psalm twenty-three. The audience, crying, was overwhelmed by the pastor's simple recitation. As the guests began to leave, the actor found the pastor and asked how he created such a powerful effect in the audience. The pastor replied, "Son, you may know acting; but I know the Shepherd."

The word *inspired* is often used to describe a play, or film, or performance like that of the retiring pastor. Inspiration produces dramatic theater beyond the scope of human knowledge and natural skill. The word *inspiration* comes from the Latin words *in* meaning *into*, and *spirare* meaning *to breath*. What exactly blows in when one is inspired? The answer is: the kingdom of God, the power of God, the spirit of God, the Holy Spirit.

The Holy Spirit's power is described by the Greek word *dunamis*, the same word that gives us *dynamite, dynamo, dynamic*. Inspiration is the work of the Holy Spirit in infusing such supernatural power into an artist, regardless of that person's belief in God, so as to provide a breakthrough, a revelation, an enlightenment, or illumination that seems to come out of nowhere. "Every good and perfect gift is from above; it comes down from the Father of all light."[17] Inspiration brought the power that fixed the Israelites' gaze on the bronze serpent; the resurrection power of God protected them from the serpent's bite.

What is this power of God's spirit? The psalmist proclaimed, "You send forth Your Spirit, they are created."[18] It is the very power that allowed Jesus to heal the lame and blind and to raise His friends from the dead. It is the power of His resurrection, "and his incomparably great power for us who believe. That power is like the working of his mighty strength, which he exerted when he raised him from the dead and seated him at his right hand in the heavenly realms."[19]

The kingdom of God breathes into the natural world. God's spirit can suspend the laws of physics. Living things are in a constant battle with the second law of thermodynamics. Dramatic artists often contend with entropy. However, so long as they can obtain enough energy, they win the battle over entropy, lifelessness, and death. They can make non-random, ordered stories, plays, and films. They expend energy to build. The Holy Spirit is a supply of living energy that never runs out. In fact, N. T. Wright, the Bishop of Durham, United kingdom, points out, "The spirit is given to make God's future real in the present."[20]

Like inspiration, the resurrection is miraculous. Like a masterpiece of the stage or screen, it doesn't seem humanly possible. The fact is, it wasn't humanly possible. The spirit of God infuses all inspired works. No wonder St. Paul called resurrection power "mighty strength." N.T. Wright notes, "Without God's Spirit, there is nothing we can do that will count for God's kingdom."[21]

God's promise is for theater artists to have this kingdom power working as they create plays and films. C.S. Lewis explained, "A car is made to run on gasoline, and it would not run properly on anything else. Now God designed the human machine to run on Himself. He Himself is the fuel our spirits were designed to burn, or the food our spirits were designed to feed on. There is no other. That is why it is just no good asking God to make us happy in our own way without bothering about religion. God cannot give us a happiness and peace apart from Himself, because it is not there. There is no such thing."[22]

The bronze serpent, like creation itself, attained its power as the future kingdom of God broke into this Present Age. Likewise, the important stories of the dramatic theater artist are by the will of God, known commonly as providence. Hamlet, the would-be dramatist, realizing "There's a divinity that shapes our ends," saw "Providence in the fall of a sparrow." Thomas Oden defines providence as "God's own act by which God orders all events in creation, nature, and history, so that the ends for which God created them will be in due time realized."[23] Providence shaped the bronze serpent and providence, here already, but not yet, shapes the important works of the dramatic theater. N. T. Wright explains this mysterious dynamic: "Somehow, God's dimension and our dimension, heaven and earth, overlap and interlock. All the questions we want to ask—How does this happen, who does it happen to, when, where, why, under what conditions, what does it look like when it does—all these remain partly mysterious, and will do until creation is finally renewed and the two spheres, the two dimensions, joined into one as they were designed to be (and as Christians pray daily that they will be)."[24]

The efficient cause of both God's creation and human dramatic theater is elusive. As J. I. Packer warns, "the truth is that God in his wisdom, to make and keep us humble and to teach us to walk by faith, has hidden from us almost everything that we should like to know about the providential purposes which he is working out."[25]

In the kingdom of God, the soul has powers available to it so far beyond our understanding that the very idea may seem foolish. Nevertheless, providence and the Holy Spirit break into our lives to empower the soul, outside the laws that govern time and space. St. Thomas Aquinas noted that, "the intellect is a power of the soul, and not the essence of the soul."[26] St. Paul tried to explain the paradox: "rather, we speak God's wisdom, mysterious, hidden, which God predetermined before the ages for our glory, and which none of the rulers of this age knew; for if they had known it, they would not have crucified the Lord of glory...We have not received the spirit of the world but the Spirit that is from God, so that we may understand the things freely given us by God. And we speak about them not with words taught by human wisdom, but with words taught by the Spirit, describing spiritual realities in spiritual terms."[27] "Let no one deceive himself. If any one among you considers himself wise in this age, let him become a fool so as to become wise."[28] "Has not God made the wisdom of the world foolish? For since in the wisdom of God the world did not come to know God through wisdom, it was the will of God through the foolishness of the proclamation to save those who have faith."[29] "For the foolishness of God is wiser than human wisdom, and the weakness of God is stronger than human strength...Not many of you were wise by human standards, not many were powerful."[30] Pascal noted, "Reason's last step is the recognition that there are an infinite number of things which are beyond it."[31]

Led by the Holy Spirit, the dramatic theater artist can seek dynamic creative power in the kingdom of

God through the cross of Jesus Christ, the fulfillment of the promise inherent in the fiery serpent. Between the Christian and all ideas, all people, and all places, stands Christ the mediator, lifted up. The cross of Christ connects the kingdom of the earthbound theater artist with the transcendent power of the kingdom of God. The theater artist lives in the kingdom of God only through His grace and through His Word, as his inspired imagination leads him to seek it. As Pope John Paul II stated, " Through his 'artistic creativity' man appears more than ever 'in the image of God'…the divine Artist passes on to the human artist a spark of his own surpassing wisdom, calling him to share in his creative power…In a very true sense it can be said that beauty is the vocation bestowed on him by the Creator in the gift of 'artistic talent.'"[32]

Without the power of the Holy Spirit invading his life, the theater artist cannot create inspired works for the stage or screen. St. Paul knew this would sound strange: "The message of the cross is foolishness to those who are perishing, but to us who are being saved it is the power of God".[33] All paths, either to the theater artists' fellow workers or to the fictive characters of a script, must lead through Christ. As theologian Dietrich Bonhoeffer wrote, "However loving and sympathetic we try to be, however sound our psychology, however frank and open our behavior, we cannot penetrate the incognito of the other man, for there are no direct relationships, not even between soul and soul. Christ stands between us, and we can only get in touch with our neighbors through him."[34]

St. Paul reminds us that, "the kingdom of God is not a matter of talk but of power."[35] And all power comes from God, not human beings. "Who confers distinction upon you? What do you possess that you have not received? But if you have received it, why are you boasting as if you did not receive it?"[36] Theater artists need to seek a breakthrough from the kingdom of God to prepare themselves to receive and transmit God's creative power.

Pascal counseled, "Be comforted; it is not from yourself that you must expect it, but on the contrary you must expect it by expecting nothing from yourself."[37] The theater artist tells God of his desires, confesses his inability to attain them with his own earth-bound human power, yields his will to His, asks Him to lead him in all his work, and thanks Him in advance. The words of Thomas A Kempis can serve as a model. He seems to be comparing the theater artist's world with the kingdom of God: "They speak most eloquently, but if You are silent, they cannot fire the heart. They instruct in the letter, but you open the understanding. They set forth the mysteries, but You reveal the meaning of all secrets...They point the way, but You grant us strength to follow it. Their action is external; You instruct and enlighten the heart. They water the seed; You make it fruitful. They proclaim the words, but You impart understanding to the mind."[38]

Every work of the dramatic theater seeks the power of the fiery serpent. We succeed in the theater in proportion to our understanding of life's experiences, our openness to invasions by the kingdom of God, and our ability to render the truth of our experiences in an engaging story that others find beneficial. Through the grace of the Holy Spirit, great plays and films reveal wisdom and joy in ways that glimpse the blessings and wonders of life in the kingdom of God.

CHAPTER 5

The Final Cause of the Dramatic Theater

The Purpose of Plays and Films How It Relates to God's Purpose in Creation

God brought the fiery serpent into being through a human artist for several reasons. First, He desired to save the Israelites from death. Second, He wanted to teach them that He was the source of their salvation. Finally, He wanted them to enjoy life in abundance in Him. These three reasons glorified God, not human beings. Artists then and today glorify God in the same way. As Pope John Paul II stated, "they must labor without allowing themselves to be driven by the search for empty glory or the craving for cheap popularity, and still less by the calculation of some possible profit for themselves."[1]

God's final cause of creation leads to the artists' final cause. John of Damascus said, "God, Who is good and more than good, did not find satisfaction in self contemplation, but in His exceeding goodness wished certain things to come into existence which would enjoy His benefits and share in His goodness. He brought all into being and created them, both what is invisible and what is visible. Yea, even man, who is a compound of the visible and the invisible."[2] Like God, the dramatic theater artist wants certain things to come about through his plays and films— the revelation of the truth, goodness, and beauty of the kingdom of God, to the glory of God.

When God broke into His story and was lifted up on the cross, He had the same goals. Jesus Christ entered the human drama at the climactic moment. He performed signs and wonders: did good—saved us from death; revealed the truth—God His father is the source of our salvation; and created beauty—modeled the path to the kingdom of God, to joy in both this life and the next. The author of the book of Hebrews tells us to "fix our eyes on Jesus, the author and perfector of our faith, who for the joy set before him endured on the cross, scorning its shame, and sat down on the right hand of God.

Consider him who endured such opposition from sinful men, so that you will not grow weary and lose heart."[3] In the kingdom of God, even suffering is transformed by Christ. Suffering becomes joy with the realization that He has atoned for our sins, drawn us closer to God, and begun to conform us to God's image. As Pascal wrote, "no one is as happy as a true Christian."

So glorious is the kingdom of God, that we seek it through the imitation of Christ, the sincerest form of flattery. God created us so that we could glorify Him. Artists who seek to imitate God's final cause, His purpose in creation, make plays and films which draw attention to our need for salvation, to the source of our salvation, and to the joy of life in the kingdom of God, "the beauty that comes from within, the unfading beauty of a gentle and quiet spirit, which is so precious to God."[4]

Joy

Joy (*chara* in the Greek) comes from the efficient cause of the dramatic theater. *Chara* is a fruit of the Spirit produced by a dynamic breakthrough of the kingdom of God. *Chara* cannot be affected by circumstance, no matter how adverse or painful. In fact, *chara* was the result of Christ's scourging and crucifixion.

Dramatic theater also produces joy both in its making and in its experiencing. Every person is hard-wired for joy. We seek it everywhere until we find it complete in the kingdom of God, where joy is multiplied in Him forever. As Karl Barth details, "It is joy in His salvation, His grace, His law, His whole action. But it is now genuine, earthly, human joy; the joy of the harvest, wedding, festival and victory; the joy not only of the inner but also of the outer man; the joy in which one may and must drink wine as well as eat bread, sing and play as well as speak, dance as well as pray."[5]

Joy comes from the making and experiencing of kingdom beauty, from the discovery and experiencing of kingdom truth, and from the doing and experiencing of kingdom goodness. Isaiah predicted, "the ransomed of the Lord shall return, and come to Zion with Singing; everlasting joy shall be upon their heads; they shall obtain joy and gladness, and sorrow and sighing shall flee away."[6] Christ fulfilled the prophet's prediction: "You have sorrow now, but I will see you again; then you will rejoice, and no one can rob you of that joy."[7]

Concern with truth, goodness, and beauty can connect the work of the dramatic theater with the kingdom of God. Our search for the kingdom of God, our seeking the Creator's power to make beauty, has provided important foundations for art and culture. George Steiner says, "In order that a man may make good use of the art he has, he needs a good will, which is perfected by moral virtue; and for this reason the Philosopher says there is a virtue of art, namely a moral virtue, in so far as the good use of art requires a moral virtue."[8]

We find truth, goodness, and beauty by trial and error. We have been given the gift of storytelling so that we might be spared the pain of learning everything personally and painfully. Plays and films let us learn truth vicariously, experiencing emotions empathetically.

Truth

God is glorified and we know joy when kingdom truth breaks into our earthly lives. Common grace, the blessings of God bestowed on all of us, allows all of us to have some grasp of His truth. All people can distinguish truth from error and grow in kingdom knowledge.

How do we know truth exists? First, we know from experience that, sought, truth has been found. Second, we know from experience that all people in all times sought truth. The word *truth* is a product of our common experience, and so enjoys a common, universal meaning. As media theorist Marshall McLuhan notes, "it is the whole basis of the mind that it seek truth, and of the soul which inspires our very life, that it seek that which gave it."[9]

All cultures believe in, value, and seek the truth. The dramatic theater is one route. Each culture may believe the truth exists in different specific applications, just as each culture may translate the same idea into their own language. Each culture conditions its members to appreciate its specific application of the truth. No culture denies the existence of truth or values falsity. Every culture considers failure to know the truth a mistake or error.

Everyone does not know the truth of the kingdom of God equally. Why? Not because of the truth, but because of something in us. When created or made things are viewed as ends in themselves, rather than as means to know and worship God, clear sight and valid understanding are obscured. When we consider ourselves, rather than God, as the center of the universe and the measure of all things, this erroneous perspective skews our vision of the kingdom of God. As Chesterton notes, "Alice must grow small if she is to be Alice in Wonderland."[10]

Truth exists in the Word of God. Jesus, the Word made flesh, declared Himself to be the truth. Kingdom truth can break into both life and into the dramatic theater through language, but primarily kingdom truth enters through people or characters. People or characters—stable, reliable, firm, trustworthy, consistent, sincere, realistic, undeceived–can reveal or embody the truth of the kingdom of God. We are drawn to kingdom people and characters in so far as they display Christlike traits; we call them protagonists or heroes.

Dramatic theater artists seeking the truth of the kingdom of God, knowing that to the extent they succeed in expressing that truth, to that extent the beauty of the kingdom of God will shine through. To seek beauty first, independent of truth, is certain to miss both beauty and truth. The truth of the kingdom of God brings blessings and leads to the path of goodness.

Goodness

When God finished his creation He said that it was good. *Good* does not mean likeable or pleasurable. Good is what God approves. Good means having the necessary qualities for its purpose; good means suitable for the reason it exists. The dramatic theater aims at some good. *Good taste* is a taste for the good; to develop good taste is to learn to like what is good. Anton Pegis observes, "When anyone endowed with an art produces bad workmanship, this is not the work of that art; in fact, it is contrary to the art."[11] To say you like a movie or play describes you; to say the movie or play is good describes it.

Common grace, the blessings of the kingdom of God bestowed on all people, allows all people to have some capacity for and appreciation of kingdom goodness. How do we know goodness exists? First, as with truth, we know from experience that, sought, kingdom goodness has been recognized. Second, we know from experience that all people in all times value and reward goodness. The word *goodness* is a product of our common experience and so enjoys a common, universal meaning.

All cultures believe in, value, and seek the good. Each culture may believe goodness exists in different specific applications, however, just as each culture may translate the same idea into their own language. Each culture conditions its members to appreciate its specific manifestations of goodness. No culture denies the existence of goodness or values evil. Every culture considers failure to do good to be a mistake or error.

St. Thomas Aquinas believed "the good of an art is to be found, not in the craftsman, but in the product…Consequently, art does not require of the craftsman that his act be a good act, but that his work be good. Rather would it be necessary for the thing made to act well (e.g., that a knife should carve well, or that a saw should cut well)…Therefore the craftsman needs art, not that he may live well, but that he may produce a good work of art, and an enduring one."[12] A good play or film glorifies God well, and blesses us, by presenting the truth of the kingdom of God.

Everyone does not understand kingdom goodness equally. Why? Not because of anything in the kingdom of God, but because of something in us. Whether created or made, if something is viewed as an end in itself, rather than as a means to know and worship God, then understanding kingdom goodness is obscured. When we consider ourselves, rather than God, as the center of the universe and the measure of all things, then this erroneous perspective skews our wisdom away from achieving kingdom goodness.

Saint Thomas Aquinas, in *The Summa Theologica*, suggests that the good of a play or film depends not on the maker's appetite (mood, emotional state, or motivation), but on the goodness of the work itself. A theater artist is valued not for the reasons the play or film is made, but for the quality of the play or film itself. Is the play or film true in the light of the kingdom of God? If so, it is good, regardless of why it was made.

A good film or play produces joy. As Pope John Paul II observed, "The link between good and beautiful stirs fruitful reflection. In a certain sense, beauty is the visible form of the good, just as good is the metaphysical condition of beauty...On this point

Plato has written: 'The power of the Good has taken refuge in the nature of the Beautiful."[13]

Beauty

Truth, goodness, and beauty proceed from the kingdom of God and are aspects of the kingdom of God. The three manifestations are intertwined characteristics of the kingdom of God: any one is insufficient; any two miss the mark; only three give us a fair concept of the reality that flows from the kingdom of God. No truth and no goodness can be enjoyed apart from beauty: in the kingdom of God, the three are interdependent. St. Thomas Aquinas believed "the beautiful is the same as the good, but with a difference of accent. Good is what all desire; therefore it is of the essence of beauty that at the knowledge and sight of it the desire is stilled... The good is that which simply pleases desire, the beautiful that which pleases on being perceived."[14] The beauty, goodness, and truth of the Present Age point us toward those of the Age to Come. As N. T. Wright explains, "The beauty of the present world is like the beauty of a chalice: it is beautiful in itself, yes, but far more beautiful because we know what it is meant to be filled with. It is like the beauty of a violin: again, beautiful in itself but still more because of the music we know it is designed to play.

Because the Spirit will one day flood the whole of creation, our task as Spirit-filled Christians in the present is to use our differing creativities to anticipate that eventual beauty, both as mission and as celebration."[15]

God disclosed the truth, goodness and beauty of the kingdom of God most completely in His Son. The cross of Christ impels us to seek it. Souls are attracted to loveliness; God made us to be irresistibly drawn to the beautiful.

When the truth and goodness of the kingdom of God is lifted up in a fiery serpent, through the cross of Jesus Christ, or in a play or film, we are compelled to stare at it, imitate it, and replicate it. King David was quite explicit: "One thing have I desired of the Lord, that will I seek after: that I may dwell in the house of the Lord all the days of my life, to behold the beauty of the Lord, and to inquire in his temple."[16] The beauty of a film or play can only be a simulation of the kingdom of God no human eye has seen because we cannot behold beauty directly. No one can see God's face and live, as Moses was instructed. Nevertheless, we can see it as in a glass darkly, a mirror dimly, on the stage, or on the screen. When kingdom beauty is near, we know in which direction to turn. "And let the beauty of the Lord our God be upon us: and establish thou the work of our hands."[17]

Beyond all human partial imitations of creation's beauty, the beauty of the kingdom of God is discerned in His creation. "Out of Zion, the perfection of beauty, God hath shined"[18] "Honour and majesty are before him: strength and beauty are in his sanctuary...O worship the Lord in the beauty of holiness: fear before him, all the earth"[19] Beauty is always related to God; it proceeds from Him. Clement of Alexandria stated, "God is the cause of everything that is beautiful"[20]

How do we know kingdom beauty exists? First, as with truth and goodness, we know from experience that, sought, kingdom beauty has been found. Second, we know from experience that all people in all times recognized beauty. The word *beauty* is a product of our common experience and so enjoys a common, universal meaning.

The critic Terry Teachout noted a desire for beauty following the attack on the World Trade center on September 11, 2001. People flocked to memorial concerts:

> "One greatly needs beauty when death is so close," old King Arkel sings in Pelleas et Melisande. Never before had I understood the meaning of those words. We wanted in our time of need beauty, and we never doubted for a moment that such a thing existed. Nor did we seek it in order to be "healed." Art isn't therapy,

just as beauty is more like bread than medicine; we need it not merely to feel better but to live, though it can also serve as a balm for scarred souls...If anything about a masterpiece can "heal" us, it...reminds us of the hidden presence of super-worldly order amid the seeming chaos of our wounded world.[21]

All cultures believe in, value, and recognize beauty. Each culture may believe that beauty exists in different specific applications, however, just as each culture may translate the same idea into their own language. Each culture conditions its members to appreciate its specific application of beauty. No culture denies the existence of beauty or values ugliness. Every culture considers the failure to recognize and appreciate beauty to be a mistake or error. The idea of beauty is another universal of our species. Thomas Oden notes, "Beauty is that quality or combination of qualities within a thing that gives pleasure to the senses or pleasurably exalts the mind or spirit. So universal is the capacity for admiration of beauty that this capacity is regarded as a normal competence of human existence, so much so that the absence of any sense of beauty would be regarded as abnormal and a diminution of human dignity."[22]

St. Augustine noted that "it is from this same supreme beauty that men who make things of beauty and love it in its outward form derive the principle by which they judge it: but they do not accept the same principle to guide them in the use they make of it. Yet it is there, and they do not see it. If only they could see it, they would not depart from it. They would preserve their strength for you, not squander it on luxuries that make them weary."[23]

Nature provides our first examples and experiences with beauty. Michelangelo claimed, "I love the beautiful human form because it is a reflection of God."[24] With God's own making, as with plays and films, beauty in unity requires the good composition of true content. Sir Archibald Russel, designer of the supersonic transport, the Concorde, believed "it so happens that our ideas of beauty are those of nature."[25]

The beauty of a play or film consists in the proportion and arrangement of the constituent parts. For example, the ancient architect Vitruvius noted the fundamental proportion of creation; nature "has created the human body in such a way that the skull from the chin to the upper brow and hairline makes up one tenth of the entire length of the body."[26] kingdom beauty always evidences simplicity, what Thomas Dubay calls "an essential purity, a freedom from superfluities, useless accretions, and needless complications."[27] kingdom beauty includes only what is necessary to create harmony (right proportion) among the parts. Aristotle asserted that "beauty consists in magnitude and ordered arrangement" and that the chief characteristics of beauty are "order, proportion, and definiteness."[28]

When the dramatic artist has given his personal experiences the form of a story that evidences a high degree of *techne*, the play or film is said to have beauty. Beauty is thus related to the skill of making. Kingdom beauty involves objective universal qualities in the form and material of the dramatic theater, related to perceptual templates in the human brain. Consequently, formal qualities that produce good structure and true content incorporate human universals, to evoke an appreciation of kingdom beauty in a play or film. When the formal and material qualities of a film or play match the brain's perceptual templates, kingdom beauty is perceived, and the work is thought to exhibit unity of form and content. As biologist Edward O. Wilson explains, "the programmed brain seeks elegance, which is the parsimonious and evocative description of pattern to make sense out of a confusion of detail."[29]

Common grace, the blessings of the kingdom of God bestowed on all people, allow all people to have some appreciation of kingdom beauty. As St. Augustine noted, "The world itself, by its well-ordered changes and movements, and by the fair appearance of all visible things, bears a testimony of its own, both that it has been created, and also that it could not have been created save by God, whose greatness and beauty are unutterable and invincible."[30]

When a dramatic story matches the universals implanted in our brains, the result radiates to us, like the light reflected by the bronze serpent. In fact, the more radiance, the more beautiful the play or film is thought to be. The kingdom of God, through the Holy Spirit, radiates as the revealed truth. Soetsu Yanagi believed "an object is truly beautiful because it belongs to the Eternal Now."[31]

Kingdom beauty means that a play or film is unified, true, and good. For example, the bronze serpent, disassembled into copper ore, tin ore, casting mold, pole, and buffing compound, would not be unified, true, or good; in fact, it would no longer be a bronze serpent. The unity that made it a bronze serpent would have been destroyed. Every element which conforms to the transcendent idea of a bronze serpent is considered true and good and unified. When the parts of a bronze serpent are united in harmony and proportion, the work attains an inner beauty. Dubay continues, "Form is the deep root of a being's actuality, which gives it its basic whatness. It is the actualizing principle of a thing, the mysterious taproot that makes that thing to be what it is, and thus why it is different from every other kind of being."[32] The inner beauty radiates outward into glory and joy, as a new creation is formed.

N. T. Wright explains, "Your own human self, your personality, your body, is being reclaimed, so that instead of being simply part of the old creation, a place of sorrow and injustice and ultimately the shame of death itself, you can be *both* part of the new creation in advance *and* someone through whom it begins to happen here and now."[33]

The inner construction and architecture also begin to explain the bronze serpent's outer characteristics—its shape, its color, its texture. Hans Urs Von Balthasar believed that "both natural forms and the forms of art have an exterior manifestation which appears and an interior depth radiating through the external aspect, neither of which, however, are separable in the form itself."[34]

Every Israelite may not have perceived the kingdom beauty of the serpent equally. Why? Not because of anything in the serpent, but because of an obstacle in the observer. When created or made things are viewed as ends in themselves, rather than means to receive the kingdom of God, sight and understanding are obscured. When we consider ourselves, rather than God, as the center of the universe and the measure of all things, this erroneous perspective skews our vision of a beautiful bronze serpent, a beautiful play, or a beautiful film.

Kingdom beauty gives joy. Beauty is "that which pleases when it is perceived" according to St. Thomas Aquinas. Kingdom beauty draws us to kingdom love. St. Augustine noted, "I used to ask my friends 'Do we love anything unless it is beautiful? What, then, is beauty and in what does it consist? What is it that attracts us and wins us over to the things we love? Unless there were beauty and grace in them, they would be powerless to win our hearts.'"[35]

Ugliness, on the other hand, is of this Evil Age. It is that which repels when it is perceived. A bronze serpent could have been ugly. An ugly bronze serpent would lack magnitude, unity, and proportion. It would be disordered, lacking truth and goodness. St. Augustine realized, "Even though it clings to things of beauty, if their beauty is outside God and outside the soul, it only clings to sorrow."[36]

Beauty can be external and internal. This Evil Age traps us with its external beauties. Von Balthasar continues, "Along with the seen surface of the manifestation there is perceived the non-manifested depth: it is only this which lends the phenomenon of the beautiful its enrapturing and overwhelming character."[37] Inner beauty, however, is of the kingdom of God. It draws people to a bronze serpent, to a film, or to a play even though its subject may be ugly. *Hamlet* and *On the Waterfront* are beautiful glimpses of the kingdom of God, even though about the Present Age's corruptions of all kinds.

Glory

In the kingdom of God, God is glorified. Glorify—*doxazo* in the Greek—comes from *doxa*, meaning *an opinion*. To glorify God means to express the opinion that God is indeed worthy of praise and honor because of His nature and His acts. By creating a play or film that reiterates this opinion, the dramatic theater artist glorifies God. The questions and answer J. I. Packer presents apply to both God and to the makers of plays and films:

> What is he after, then? What is his goal? What does he aim at? When he made us, his purpose was that we should love and honor him, praising him for the wonderfully ordered complexity and variety of his world, using it according to his will, and so enjoying both it and him. His immediate objectives are to draw individual men and women into a relationship of faith, hope, and love toward himself, delivering them from sin and showing forth in their lives the power of his grace; to defend his people against the forces of evil; and to spread throughout the world the gospel by means of which he saves.[38]

All of creation, including the dramatic theater, has the same purpose—to glorify God. This fact gives creation, plays, and films, Kingdom significance; we and the films and plays we make are meaningful to God. Pastor Tim Keller describes the relationship between meaning and glory:

> What does *meaning* mean? How do we define *meaning*? Significance is really a synonym but it does not capture all that is contained in the word *meaning*. Can we define *meaning*? I believe we can. While it appears to some to be almost impossible to define, yet it is clearly something we know exists and understand at some level. Even people who insist that nothing has any meaning show that they don't believe their own words when they don't live as people who have no meaning. Many people do not know what it is that gives meaning to life but they know intuitively that life is meaningful. What I have found is that the meaning of life is the glory of God. All meaning is some aspect of the glory of God. If there is no God then nothing can have ultimate significance. The word *glory* means weight, it means significance—it basically means *meaning*.[39]

We can discover the meaning of living, of making for and through God, by seeking His kingdom, delighting in God, and enjoying the Already/Not Yet world He has made for us. Jesus says, "I came that they might have life, and have it abundantly" (John 10:10).

In knowing God, enjoying life in abundance in the kingdom of God, the artists of the dramatic theater find joy unmatchable which blesses every part of their lives. God is the source of all joy. Joy encompasses both profound experiences of pleasure and simple satisfaction with one's life. Joy is lasting satisfaction, complete, touching the whole of the artist's life. Joy means the peace of doing good work, making beautiful films and plays, and knowing the work is true. Kingdom joy, true happiness, lies only in the kingdom of God. Chesterton says, "The perfect happiness of men on the earth (if it ever comes) will not be a flat and solid thing, like the satisfaction of animals. It will be an exact and perilous balance; like that of a desperate romance. Man must have just enough faith in himself to have adventures, and just enough doubt of himself to enjoy them."[40]

Pope John Paul II summarizes the task of the theater artist making plays and films:

Human beings, in a certain sense, are unknown to themselves—Jesus Christ not only reveals God but "fully reveals man to man." In Christ, God has reconciled the world to himself. All believers are called to bear witness to this; but it is up to you, men and women who have given your lives to art, to declare with all the wealth of your ingenuity that in Christ the world is redeemed; the human person is redeemed, the human body is redeemed, and the whole creation which, according to Saint Paul, "awaits impatiently the revelation of the child of God" is redeemed. The creation awaits the revelation of the children of God also through art and in art. This is your task. Humanity in every age, and even today, looks to works of art to shed light upon its path and its destiny.[41]

Every film and play has the same purpose as all of creation—to glorify God by redeeming His children by leading them to His kingdom. All of creation points to the kingdom of God, just as every play and film points to something about the age in which the artist lived. The theater artist, himself an indicator of his creator, draws attention by seeking the kingdom of God.

Some dramatic theater can show a person seeking the kingdom of God, experiencing an unmatched intensity of joy, discovering that his life has a purpose in God, acting in ways that fulfill his God-given purpose, and living joyfully and eternally. "The Lord your God will bless you in all your harvest and in all the work of your hands, and your joy will be complete."[42] Characters may consciously or unconsciously seek the kingdom by following Jesus Christ; the cross is their axis and compass.

On the other hand, some films and plays show people, consciously or unconsciously, living in this Present Evil Age under the rule of the Prince of Darkness, seeking joy apart from God, acting in ways which run counter to His purpose, and pursuing the material life of the earthly kingdom as a substitute for eternal life in the kingdom of God. These characters believe and tell lies, deceive and are deceived, fear and cause fear, tempt and yield to temptation.

Many plays and films echo the lesson learned painfully by Job. Stripped of everything he values, Job demands to know why. George Steiner thought, "in his lunatic suffering, Job demands to know the purpose of creation, the intention of the builder. The clay made abject, turns on the potter."[43]

"God's address to Job comes out of an artist's workshop."[44] The creator refuses to justify or explain himself to his creation. The potter refuses to hold himself accountable to the clay. God's explanation to Job is God's answer to Moses: "I am what I am." Job learns along with both theater artists and many characters in films and plays, painfully. Job learns not to ask why, but rather to praise God and seek His will; many theater artists and characters do not learn this lesson. When Job learns the truth, and does good, he encounters the kingdom of God. When the theater artist presents the truth in a good and beautiful film or play, both he and his audience encounter the kingdom of God. And God is glorified. As Nehemiah proclaimed, "Do not grieve, for the joy of the Lord is your strength."[45]

CHAPTER 6

The Working Christian Theater Artist

What it is like to be a Christian Theater Artist

The American theater critic George Jean Nathan half-jokingly referred to the theater as the house of Satan. Anyone just glancing at a supermarket tabloid would be inclined to agree. Theater and film seem trapped in this Evil Age. Throughout history, the dramatic theater has been home to the latest challenges to traditional beliefs and values and to the current fashions in belief and living. Since the age of the apostle Timothy, the times have been hostile to the creative work of the Christian: "There will be very difficult times. For people will love only themselves and their money.

They will be boastful and proud, scoffing at God, disobedient to their parents, and ungrateful. They will consider nothing sacred. They will be unloving and unforgiving; they will slander others and have no self-control; they will be cruel and have no interest in what is good. They will betray their friends, be reckless, be puffed up with pride, and love pleasure rather than God."[1]

The ethics of life in the dramatic theater could be summarized in a version of Christ's most famous sermon:

> Happy are the "pushers": for they get on in the world.
> Happy are the hard-boiled: for they never let life hurt them.
> Happy are they who complain; for they get their own way in the end.
> Happy are the blasé: for they never worry over their sins.
> Happy are the slave drivers: for they get results.
> Happy are the knowledgeable men of the world: for they know their way around.
> Happy are the troublemakers: for they make people take notice of them[2]

St. Paul urged the Christian artist, "Do not conform yourselves to this age but be transformed by the renewal of your mind, that you may discern what is the will of God, what is good and pleasing and perfect."[3] In the paradigm of the bronze serpent, the work of art is transformed and lifted up for all to see amid thousands of poisonous snakes killing people left and right. Like the Israelite bronze sculptor, the Christian artist working in film and theater inhabits the two worlds identified by St Augustine in the fifth century—the City of Man and the City of God, the Present Age and the Age to Come, this Evil Age and the kingdom of God.

Christians making plays and films must negotiate the dynamic tension between the two worlds. On one side is the kingdom of applause, human fame, great wealth, unimaginable pleasures, and public acclaim—contemporary poisonous serpents. On the other side is the kingdom of God, the path of the master creator with its servanthood of obedience, persecution, meekness, and hungering and thirsting after righteousness. The theater artist who lives out his faith to the full is tested to the full.

Love

Into what kind of a person does faith in Christ shape the Christian making films and plays? He becomes a person who seeks first the kingdom of God, who trusts and obeys the power of God as revealed by His Word, who believes in the living incarnation of Jesus Christ, and who lives and works by the guidance of the Holy Spirit. "The only thing that counts is faith expressing itself through love."[4] This is the spiritual reality that should fill the Christian and manifest itself to the world in his life making films and plays. For the Christian, the dramatic theater is a sacramental response of love to his God revealed in Jesus Christ. The Christian theater artist lovingly abandons himself to God, and from his place in the kingdom of God prepares to act, to make, to create. Writer Tony Hendra recalled how his Father Joe explained the theater artist's work as prayer: "The work itself is prayer. Work done as well as possible. Work done for others first and yourself second. Work you are thankful for. Work you enjoy, that uplifts you. Work that celebrates existence, whether it's growing grain in the fields or using God-given skills like yours. All this is prayer that binds us together and therefore to God."[5]

Every one of the theater artist's acts bears witness to the glory of the kingdom of God. As Pope John Paul II noted, "There is therefore an ethic, even a 'spirituality' of artistic service, which contributes in its way to the life and renewal of a people."[6]

Jesus said, "You shall love the Lord, your God, with all your heart, with all your soul, and with all your mind. This is the greatest and the first commandment. The second is like it: You shall love your neighbor as yourself."[7] God measures the theater artists' love first by their obedience to His commands. Jesus said, "Those who love me will keep my word."[8] Obedience is aligning one's life with His commands. God knows how hard theater artists find it to obey in the circumstances of movie and play making. He hears when they claim either ignorance of His commands or misunderstanding. He knows when they do not have the courage or the strength to obey

Jesus' disciples enjoyed the personal guidance of Christ Himself for three years. Theater artists are unable to converse with Him as the disciples did and receive an audible answer for their creative and professional questions. But theater artists have the benefit of His presence; the day before He was crucified, Christ promised the disciples that He would not leave them alone in a world of poisonous snakes. He pledged to send them a helper, the Holy Spirit, to guide them as a stage or film director might.

The Holy Spirit today can reveal to the makers of films and plays the truth, the goodness, and the beauty of the kingdom of God in any and all circumstances. He can enable producers and grips alike to walk in the way that He reveals. He also can correct their courses when they stray. God's kingdom is not the theater or film world's kingdom. But as N. T. Wright observes, "the point of the Spirit is to enable those who follow Jesus to take into all the world the news that he is Lord, that he has won the victory over the forces of evil, that a new world has opened up and that we are to help make it happen."[9]

Satan is the prince of this earth, and throughout history the dramatic theater has been the prince's playground. The enemy attempts to camouflage his films and plays with high principles, altruistic goals, and social justifications to confuse people. Director Mel Gibson felt the spiritual warfare on the set while filming *The Passion of the Christ*:

> The big realms are slugging it out. We're just the meat in the sandwich. And for some reason we're worth it. I don't know why, but we are...Complications happened to block certain things, and the closer you are to a breakthrough point, the more vigorous it gets, so that you know when the opposition is at its greatest, you're close and you have to keep pressing on. That happened a number of times [in production], and it's happened a number of times since...Production was tough. Post-production has been brutal. You name it, it's happened...Whoa, the world goes into revolt.[10]

The Holy Spirit is the Christian artist's guide in the Evil Age's wilderness of poisonous snakes. The Holy Spirit always responds to the prayers and faith of Christians making plays and films. The Spirit can even break into a production of a secular movie, like *On the Waterfront*, transforming it into a parable of redemption. On the other hand, a film like *The Last Temptation of Christ*, can leave its screenwriter, Paul Schrader seeking an explanation for its poor reception among Christians: "All I was trying to do was provoke discussion about Christ.... [W]hen I was at Calvin College, we were encouraged to discuss views of Christ that didn't necessarily match our own."[11]

While seeking the kingdom of God, the artists of the dramatic theater hear a "still, small voice" within when confronted with situations or decisions that could take their work outside the will of God.

Obedience

God commands, "You shall love the Lord your God." In making a play or a film, the theater artist encounters many people giving him instructions, making demands on him, planning his days, requesting compliance, issuing orders, presenting temptations, and rationalizing and justifying all sorts of things. For the Christian, all of these human messages must be filtered through the cross of Christ and found consistent with life in the kingdom of God.

Most contemporary discussions of obedience are framed by the adjective *blind* as in, *blind obedience*.

But Christian obedience is anything but blind. In fact, the Holy Spirit explains the ultimate script, Scripture, so that theater artists cannot claim they have misunderstood it. He is the ultimate producer and director, reminding theater artists of His commands as they make films and plays. What's more, the Spirit of God strengthens and comforts theater artists when faced with inevitable difficulties in seeking the kingdom of God while living in the house of Satan. Christian screenwriter Steve Tompkins discusses the challenges writing a hit television series: "At *The Simpsons* you are reined in. You can't stick your neck out and do anything that's overtly religious on its face. You must undercut it. There's a gag reflex in comedy writers to undercut any honest religious sentiment. It is easier to pass a camel through the eye of a needle than it is to make a comedy writer quote Scripture with a straight face."[12]

Christian obedience means wide-eyed compliance: first, to the plan of God; first, to the pattern of Christ; first, to His kingdom rules; first, to His kingdom standard; and first, to His will. Only then does the Christian artist consider compliance to a producer's plan, a designer's pattern, an agent's rules, a union's standard, or a casting director's will. Obedience to Christ is the bottom line in the Christian artist's life on stage or in the studio.

Basic to every decision made in making a film or a play is knowing what Scripture says about an issue, knowing what action God wants taken, knowing what attitude would please Him, and knowing the required steps. Obedience is following God's timing of a career in film or on the stage, and His manner of bringing it to fruition. It has been said, God may not come when we want, but He is never late, and nothing makes God laugh as much as hearing our plans.

Just as a camera operator or an actor cannot follow a director's command without knowing it, the Christian theater artist cannot follow God's commands without knowing them. And as the camera operator or actor may ask for clarification from the director, so the Christian theater artist asks the Holy Spirit for both help in relating God's commands to a particular situation and assistance in determining the wisest course of action.

When a Christian theater artist decides to seek the kingdom of God, he can expect Satan to challenge the course of action. Mel Gibson's *The Passion of the Christ* was attacked even before it was shot. Satan doesn't want a filmmaker or playmaker to seek the kingdom of God; he may suggest shortcuts and raise doubts to divert the work away from God's direction or to weaken the product through small steps of compromise. Christian theater artists counter the enemy's challenges by resolving to follow the lordship of Jesus Christ and by invoking the power of His blood and word. To work on a film or a play with the same commitment with which Christ went to the cross, requires obedient action, a determined attitude, a willingness to suffer any consequence, and an abiding in the Father. The Word of God promises the power to confront the problems Satan may create. Each kingdom offers its own set of lenses:

The Present Evil Age	*The kingdom of God*
It's impossible	All things are possible[13]
I'm confused	I will direct your path[14]
I'm not able	I am able[15]
I'm not strong enough	I will strengthen you[16]
I can't manage	I will supply your needs[17]
It's too much for me	I will help you[18]
I'm worried	I'll take your worries[19]
I'm too tired	I will give you rest[20]
It's not worth it	It will be worth it[21]
Nobody loves me	I will always love you[22]
I'm afraid	I will give you peace[23]

God requires His servants to seek His perspective for each day's creative work, on every aspect of the creative process. The Christian artist daily renews his mind so his attitude and actions honor Him. The Christian artist sees sad examples around him of who we are apart from Christ. Yet even with

His perspective, the Christian rehearsing a play or making a film needs courage: courage to give up what is pleasurable in the short term for long term joy; courage to do things which may upset collaborators; courage to follow a schedule which matches His plan; courage to love the unlovely fellow artist, to forgive the unforgivable action, and to give up to another what he wants to keep for himself. "Therefore, as God's chosen people, holy and dearly loved, clothe yourselves with compassion, kindness, humility, gentleness and patience. Bear with each other and forgive whatever grievances you may have against one another. Forgive as the Lord forgave you. And over all these virtues put on love, which binds them all together in perfect unity. Let the peace of Christ rule in your hearts, since as members of one body you were called to peace. And be thankful."[24] Courage amid poisonous snakes in the house of Satan grows from a deepening walk into the kingdom of God.

As the Christian theater artist comes to experience the kingdom of God more intimately, confidence in Him increases, and obedience in working on a film or play becomes easier. If an actor or a camera operator knows the God who gives the commands, then he'll be more apt to trust that His plans are for his good and His glory. He will rely on the Holy Spirit first, and not as a last resort, knowing

He guides him best. By following the Savior Jesus Christ instead of following his billing, salary, or perks, the Christian theater artist can work boldly, without fearing the immediate consequences that may arise, always looking forward to the blessings of God's kingdom. As St. Paul urged Timothy, "Be diligent to present yourself approved to God as a workman who does not need to be ashamed, accurately handling the word of truth."[25]

Like all obedience in the dramatic theater, Christian obedience to God is learned by trial and error. Every artist is naturally rebellious. Obedience to, and trust in, the one in charge must be learned. Childlike innocence and faith are often nurtured in the training of artists for the stage and screen. But only after the theater artist is born-again into new life in the kingdom of God and set free from slavery to childish rebellion and feelings can a heart-felt desire to obey God emerge.

In long rehearsal periods or production schedules, artists sometimes wonder if things are going the right way. The Christian theater artist is not immune to similar doubts. Though God may reveal His kingdom, the way into it isn't always clear. Obedience requires the Christian theater artist to respond to the Spirit's lead, even when the details are unknown.

In order to make obedience real in his film and theater work, the Christian artist must learn several things. First, he needs to develop the ability to wait on God in prayer. "Devote yourselves to prayer, being watchful and thankful."[26] Prayer is to be *active waiting*, like an actor's *active listening*, during which the theater artist learns, examines, and understands what He is asking. Writer Tony Hendra notes the similarity of the listening he learned in the improvisational work of Second City and Father Joe's explanation of the listening required of God:

> The only way to know God, the only way to know the other, is to listen. Listening is reaching out into that unknown other self, surmounting your walls and theirs; listening is the beginning of understanding, the first exercise of love. "None of us listen enough, do we, dear? We only listen to a fraction of what people say. It's a wonderfully useful thing to do. You almost hear something you didn't expect...No question that there were startling parallels between what the fathers of improv and Father Joe had to say. Between Second City and the City of God.[27]

Director Mel Gibson says that when an artist neglects prayer, "you fall into chaos."[28] Director Tom Shadyac agrees:

> I pray because it's essential for me. I have come to view prayer as a conversation....I've come to

believe that prayer can be so many things. I read, write and pray in the mornings. My writing, my journaling, became a form of prayer, being honest with God. 'I'm frustrated with this.' 'What's happening here?' And, 'I feel sad about that'...We should live our lives as 24/7 forms of prayer, offering our lives completely. To me that's the goal. As the theater artist practices prayerful listening, he learns to recognize His voice. To hear, the Christian theater artist must resist outside pressure, exercise self-control, and wait.[29]

Second, the theater artist working in film or theater needs to meditate upon the Word of God by asking questions like, "What do these verses teach me about God's will for this current project?" "Is there an example here to follow or avoid today in this rehearsal or shoot?" "Is this a command, a promise, or a warning that I need to apply to my current challenge?" "What do I need to do to align my work today with this truth?" The Word of God is power.

These two spiritual disciplines—waiting in prayer and meditating on Scripture— are the twin foundations of the creative life and work of the Christian working in film or theater. If either foundation is weak, the Christian's creative work may not fulfill the purpose God has for it. A strong foundation is necessary for the inevitable trouble.

Obedience to Christ in the worlds of the stage and screen will most likely bring conflict. Challenges arise when Christian artists are asked to do something contrary to God's plan. There may be conflict between God's kingdom values and those of the director's interpretation of a script. Christ promised His followers a path of conflict and persecution. Finally, to learn obedience, the Christian theater artist must willingly accept chastisement. Eric Ellenbogen, the Chief Executive Officer of Classic Media, believes "sometimes having a huge success is the worst thing that can happen. You start to believe you have a secret formula for making movies that no one else has. Then you make a second feature, and it's a flop and you lose everything. There is no secret formula."[30] God, out of His great love, allows His theater workers the pain of discipline, and even of failure, so that they may turn back to Him.

On the other hand, the Christian life in the kingdom of God also includes submitting to the authorities making the film or play. God has deliberately given some people, even non-Christian people, jurisdiction over Christian theater artists, so that Christians making plays and films can learn what it means to obey. Christian theater artists practice surrendering their personal desires, even when they do not understand, or when the cost seems too high.

Joyful laughter characterizes the creative process. The Christian theater artist does not want to miss the blessings the Lord has planned for those doing His will on stage and screen. But theater artists are always faced with choices in the making of a film or play. The choices they make sometimes end up sacrificing the future blessings God had prepared for the immediate "blessings" at hand.

Israel, puffed up and stiff necked, wandered in the desert for forty years, even after seeing the fiery serpent, because they were afraid to enter the Promised Land, the image of the kingdom of God. Though the Israelites were on the brink of tremendous blessing, they lost the outpouring of God's goodness by their stubbornness and self-reliance. The Christian in film and theater, on the other hand, seeks a life of surrender and obedience, not independence and rebellion. To live such a life means bringing every choice to the Lord and then listening and accepting His answers

Obedience to God in the world of the theater and film can seem foolish at times. But such foolishness allows God to demonstrate His kingdom power. God becomes the only available explanation to choices that defy human reason yet prove successful–signs and wonders. One of the most foolish choices Christ asks of the theater artist is to put his fellow worker above himself, to be his servant.

Servanthood

Loving God through obedience to His commands is but the first part of kingdom living in the dramatic theater. The second part of God's great command is even more difficult—"And your neighbor as yourself." Loving God means obedience to Him. People in and around the dramatic theater express love in many ways. Some buy gifts or give awards, some lavish words of praise, some follow the artists' every word and deed, some try to just touch their favorite artist. Christians choose acts of service.

Jesus asked, "For who is greater, the one who reclines at the table or the one who serves?"[31] He answered, "Whoever wishes to become great among you shall be your servant."[32] The Christian making films or plays is called by Christ to adopt a servant-hearted attitude. Everyone involved in making a play or film can thereby see Christ in the Christian artist as he serves, as he gives, as he yields, as he endures, as he rejoices. In making a play or film, the Christian artist follows John Wesley's Rule: "Do all the good you can, in all the ways you can, to all the souls you can, in every place you can, at all the times you can, with all the zeal you can, as long as ever you can."[33] The Christian theater artist believes, "But whatever things were gain to me, those things I have counted as loss for the sake of Christ. More than that, I count all things to be loss in view of the surpassing value of knowing Christ Jesus my Lord, for whom I have suffered the loss of all things, and count them but rubbish so that I may gain Christ,"[34]

The theater artist's heart attitude—growing from seeking the kingdom of God first—is the most important prerequisite to his service to both God and his neighbors in the production. Martin Luther explained, "God judges according to what is at the bottom of the heart, and for this reason, His law makes its demands on the inmost heart and cannot be satisfied with works, but rather punishes works that are done otherwise than from the bottom of the heart."[35] The motivation for servanthood is paramount: "You are those who justify yourselves in the sight of men, but God knows your hearts; for that which is highly esteemed among men is detestable in the sight of God."[36] The Christian working in film and on the stage does not just give help graciously, he also receives help graciously. "Dear friends, since God so loved us, we also ought to love one another. No one has ever seen God; but if we love one another, God lives in us and his love is made complete in us."[37]

The Christian theater artist lays his humanity open, transparent for all to see. He is certainly not perfect, and he does not try to appear to be so. In fact, the Christian making films and plays is open about his imperfection. Director Mel Gibson's own anti-Semitism surfaced years after *The Passion of the Christ* opened. The Christian theater artist readily admits his defects and flaws to his co-workers and is not ashamed to ask for their help or forgiveness. "Not that I have already obtained it or have already become perfect, but I press on so that I may lay hold of that for which also I was laid hold of by Christ Jesus."[38] Christians in authority, like the producer and director, need humility. As Chesterton noted, "the man should rule who does not think that he can rule."[39]

The Christian making a film or a play is vulnerable; he can admit and discuss his mistakes and failures. His only concern for reputation is for how Christ views his work. Even the director of a film or a play needs vulnerability. Director Elia Kazan believed the director needs, "the ability to say, 'I am wrong,' or 'I was wrong.' Not as easy as it sounds. But in many situations, these three words, honestly spoken will save the day. They are the words, very often, that the actors struggling to give the director what he wants, most need to hear from him. Those words, 'I was wrong, let's try it another way,' the ability to say them can be a life-saver."[40]

Ultimately, the mission of Jesus was to destroy the activity of Satan in the world and establish the kingdom of God. The spiritual warfare continues today in the lives of every Christian theater artist working in the Present Evil Age, but living with the dynamic tension in God's Already But Not Yet kingdom. The universal bent toward sin, the biases of a particular culture, and the prejudices of one's family can allow strongholds to be planted which can later thwart the artist's efforts to advance the kingdom. When the artist does stumble or fall into dependency on alcohol, drugs, or sex, the world waits to see how the Christian responds. For example, Mel Gibson announced "I have begun an ongoing programme of recovery and what I am now realizing is that I cannot do it alone....I am asking the Jewish community, whom I have personally offended, to help me on my journey through recovery."[41] Through the Holy Spirit, God offers the journey of forgiveness, redemption, and recovery, not just to fictional characters, but to artists as well: "Forget the former things; do not dwell on the past. See, I am doing a new thing! Now it springs up; do you not perceive it? I am making a way in the desert and steams in the wasteland."[42]

The Christian theater artist displays a genuine humility. He is not defensive when criticized or asked to do something. The Christian making films and plays has an authentic desire to help his fellow artists, either when asked or after asking. Like a good servant, the Christian making a film or rehearsing a play continually looks for ways to serve and give of himself, humbly and inconspicuously. He willingly hides his strengths and reveals his weaknesses. Howard Butt says, "Christ's death frees you from hiding your sins. You can be vulnerable and open. When you are weak then you are strong. You shake the darkness with irresistible blows; the divine might of weakness. You hit your hardest when your guard is down."[43] He witnesses for Christ primarily by his actions, reserving his words as a last resort. "Be wise in the way you act toward outsiders; make the most of every opportunity. Let your conversation be always full of grace, seasoned with salt, so that you may know how to answer everyone."[44] Marshall McLuhan advised, "There is no need to mention Christianity. It is enough that it be known that the operator is a Christian."[45]

The Christian theater artist is absolutely honest, but kind. His candor has neither ulterior motive nor hidden meaning. The hypocrisy, duplicity, and game playing which occasionally characterize the making of plays and films have no part in his life. The Christian is real. Phil Vischer, the creator of *VeggieTales*, explains the filmmaking demise: "I was trying to be someone that God didn't call me to be and that God didn't create me to be. It wasn't working, and I couldn't see a way out without disappointing a lot of people."[46] The Christian artist making a film or play seeks the meekness and gentleness of Christ, which means he is soothing, tender, polite, tactful, courteous, and respectful to his collaborators. "Do all things without grumbling or disputing; so that you will prove yourselves to be blameless and innocent, children of God above reproach in the midst of a crooked and perverse generation, among whom you appear as lights in the world, holding fast the word of life."[47]

The Christian theater artist's servant heart must not be confused with a poor self-image, insecurity, or fawning. The Christian making a film or play has healthy self-esteem, but not to the point of selfishness or egotism. "Whoever boasts, should boast in the Lord. For it is not the one who recommends himself who is approved, but the one whom the Lord recommends."[48]

Unlike the American philosopher Ralph Waldo Emerson's self-reliant person, the Christian theater artist has confidence in himself as a new creation in the kingdom of God: "I can do all things through Him who strengthens me."[49] His spiritual maturity leads him to seek the kingdom of God more and more, as his artistic maturity leads him to depend less and less on his earthly mentors. In the kingdom of God he is not easily crippled, wounded, or discouraged by either his creative process or the reviews of his work "You have taken off your old self with its practices and have put on the new self, that is being renewed in knowledge in the image of its Creator."[50]

In a world of ego and self-promotion, the Christian theater artist battles pride constantly. Chesterton notes, "One can hardly think too little of one's self. One can hardly think too much of one's soul."[51] In fact, the proof of the Christian theater artist's servanthood is his voluntary and personal anonymity and generosity. The Christian working in theater and film does not seek to advance his career; he seeks to advance the kingdom of God. "Do nothing from selfishness or empty conceit, but with humility of mind regard one another as more important than yourselves; do not merely look out for your own personal interests, but also for the interests of others. Have this attitude in yourselves which was also in Christ Jesus."[52] As record producer Charlie Peacock writes, Christian artists "pursue greatness in craft in order to give the Lord the best fruit of the talent he has given them, not to build themselves up. They understand that true greatness is found in the heart of the servant."[53]

In rehearsal, the Christian artist looks vertically for favor and guidance not horizontally to his peers. "Whatever you do, work at it with all your heart, as working for the Lord, not for men."[54] As Henri Nouwen said, "In order to be of service to others we have to die to them; that is, we have to give up measuring our meaning and value with the yardstick of others...thus, we become free to be compassionate."[55]

When he does look across at his coworkers, the Christian film or theater artist simply grieves for those outside the kingdom of God. As a bronze serpent, the Christian making films and plays reflects the light. His function is not to attract attention and people to himself, but to the source of his light: Jesus Christ. Christian filmmaking and playmaking can be breakthroughs of the kingdom of God into the dark places both in the world and in the human heart, so that Christ may heal each.

The Christian theater artist is also a peacemaker. First, he is at peace with himself as He abides in Christ. Second, he is a vehicle for the peace of Christ to settle quarrels and to restore relationships. The Christian making a play or a film builds up rather than tears down. In a world of hard language and biting, often cruel, humor, the Christian artist watches his tongue, speaking to heal not to hurt. In a world of great passion and temper, he is slow to anger: "You must rid yourselves of all such things as these: anger, rage, malice, slander, and filthy language from your lips. Do not lie to each other."[56] The great Christian educator John Cardinal Newman gives the Christian theater artist a working creed: "God has created me to do Him some definite service; He has committed some work to me which he has not committed to another. I have my mission. Therefore I will trust Him. Whatever, wherever I am, I can never be thrown away. If I am in sickness, my sickness may serve Him; in perplexity, my perplexity may serve Him; if I am in sorrow, my sorrow may serve Him. My sickness, or perplexity, or sorrow may be necessary causes of some great end, which is quite beyond us. He does nothing in vain."[57]

So what does it mean to be a Christian theater artist working in the world of stage and film? It means that men and women, isolated in time and space, armed with the power of the Holy Spirit, seek to imitate the creative life of the God of the universe, take their human experiences and, through prayer and meditation, transform their personal lives into a meaningful universal story of redemption, pointing all who see or hear it to the kingdom of God—the glory of God and the joy of life now and forever. Through the power of the Holy Spirit and by the grace of God, Christians working on stage and before the camera can transform humanity's aesthetic experiences into religious experiences, as the life that had been a mystery is saved by the actual experience of the living God. N.T. Wright suggests, "The Spirit is given so that we, ordinary mortals that we are, can ourselves be, in a measure, what Jesus himself was: part of God's future arriving in the present; a place where heaven and earth meet; the means of God's kingdom going forwards."[58] The stage and the screen become our bronze and fiery serpents.

Endnotes

Preface

[1] Denby, David. *Great Books. My Adventures with Homer, Rousseau, Woolf, and Other Indestructible Writers of the Western World* (New York: Simon and Schuster, 1996).

[2] MacArthur, John, ed. *The MacArthur Study Bible* (Nashville: Word Bibles, 1997).

[3] Psalm 104: 3-34, New King James Version.

Chapter 1

[1] Numbers, 21 6-9 New American Standard Bible.

[2] 2 Kings 18: 4-7 New American Standard Bible.

[3] For a full discussion see George Eldon Ladd's *The Gospel of the Kingdom. Scriptural Studies in the Kingdom of God.* (Grand Rapids: W. W. Eerdmans Publishing Company, 1959).

[4] Godawa, Brian. *Hollywood Worldviews. Watching Films with Wisdom and Discernment* (Downers Grove, Illinois: InterVarsity Press, 2002) 13.

[5] Maritian, Jacques. *Art and Scholasticism* (New York: Charles Scribner's Sons, 1947) 62.

[6] Beckerman, Bernard. *Dynamics of Drama. Theory and Method of Analysis* (New York: Drama Book Specialists (Publishers), 1979) 10, 20.

[7] Exodus 35:32.

[8] Wisdom of Solomon 16: 5-12. The New Jerusalem Bible (New York: Doubleday, 1990) 802.

[9] Psalm 111: 2.

[10] Maritain, *Art and Scholasticism*, 53.

[11] John 14:6 New International Version Bible

Chapter Two

[1] McKee, Robert. *Story. Substance, Structure, Style and the Principles of Screenwriting* (New York: Regan Books: 1997) 113.

[2] Bogdanovich, Peter. *Who the Devil Made It* (New York: Ballentine Books, 1997) 375.

[3] "Mel Gibson on his Passion: Jesus Christ" in *HOLLYWOOD JESUS NEWSLETTER Number 53 Pop Culture From A Spiritual Point of View*, April 23, 2003

<http://www.hollywoodjesus.com/newsletter053.htm>.

4 Humphrey, Nicholas. *A History of the Mind.* (New York: Simon and Schuster, 1992) 101.

5 Ibid.

6 Hall, Donald. *Writing Well.* (Boston: Little, Brown and Company, 1973) 212.

7 Chesterton, G.K. *Orthodoxy* (New York: Image Books, 1959) 59.

8 Ibid., 78.

9 Tolkien, J.R.R. *The Lord of the Rings* (New York: Houghton Mifflin Company, 1994) 697.

10 Kazan, Elia. *A Life* (New York: Doubleday, 1989) 528.

11 "Interview with Tom Shadyac. Director of Bruce Almighty" in *HOLLYWOOD JESUS NEWSLETTER Number 56 Pop Culture From A Spiritual Point of View* May 24, 2003, <http://www.hollywoodjesus.com/newsletter056.htm>.

12 Field, Syd. *The Screenwriter's Workbook* (New York: Dell Publishing, 1984) 17.

13 Ibid., 19.

14 Sayers, Dorothy. *The Mind of the Maker.* (New York: Harper and Row, 1941) 39.

15 From a speech by Elia Kazan, Wesleyan University, Middletown, Connecticut, 1973.

16 Ciment, Michel. *Kazan on Kazan* (New York: Viking Press, 1974), 105.

17 Ecclesiastes 3:14. New American Standard Bible, updated.

[18] Ecclesiastes 3:11. New American Standard Bible, updated.

[19] Bogdanovich, *Who the Devil Made It,* 60.

[20] Ibid., 61.

[21] Dionysus, *Divine Names,* trans. by C.E. Rolt. (London: S.P.C.K.: 1975), Volume VIII, Section 7, 158.

[22] Bogdanovich, *Who the Devil Made It,* 531.

[23] Chesterton, *Orthodoxy,* 116.

[24] Witt, Jonathan, "The Gods Must Be Tidy! Is the Cosmos a Work of Poor Engineering or the Gift of an Artistic Designer?" *Touchstone* Volume 17, Number 6, 30.

[25] Ibid.

[26] Ibid.

[27] Ibid.

[28] Wilson, Edward O. *Consilience: The Unity of Knowledge* (New York: Alfred A. Knopf: 1998) 55.

[29] Bogdanovich, *Who the Devil Made It,* 416.

[30] Dissanayake, Ellen. *Homo Aestheticus: Where Art Comes from and Why* (Seattle: University of Washington Press, 1995) 55.

[31] Ibid., 92.

[32] Steiner, George. *Grammars of Creation* (New Haven: Yale University Press, 2001) 33.

[33] Packer, J.I. *Knowing God.* (Downers Grove, Illinois: InterVarsity Press, 1973) 56.

[34] McKee, *Story. Substance, Structure, Style and the Principles of Screenwriting*

[35] Chesterton, *Orthodoxy,* 143.

[36] Percy, Walker, "How to be an American Novelist in Spite of Being Southern and Catholic" *Signposts in a*

Strange Land (New York: Farrar, Straus and Giroux, 1991) 178.

[37] McLuhan, Marshall. "Catholic Humanism and Modern Letters", *The Medium and the Light: Reflections on Religion* (Toronto: Stoddart Publishing Company Ltd., 1999) 169.

[38] Morphew, Derek J. *Breakthrough: Discovering the Kingdom* (Capetown: Vineyard International Publishing, 1998) 77.

[39] Chesterton, *Orthodoxy*, 143.

[40] Ibid., 36.

[41] Lewis, C.S. *Mere Christianity*. (New York: Macmillan Company Publishing, 1952) 146-47.

[42] Ibid., 167.

[43] Ibid., 142.

[44] Godawa, Brian. *Hollywood Worldviews. Watching Films with Wisdom and Discernment,* 15.

[45] Bogdanovich, *Who the Devil Made It*, 489.

[46] Lewis, C.S. *The Allegory of Love* (New York: Oxford University Press, 1959) 44.

[47] Pope John Paul II, "Letter of His Holiness Pope John Paul II to Artists", 1999.

[48] Sayers, Dorothy. *The Mind of the Maker,* 39.

[49] Steiner, *Grammars of Creation*, 263.

[50] Percy, Walker. "The State of the Novel: Dying Art or New Science?" *Signposts in a Strange Land* (New York: Farrar, Straus and Giroux: 1991) 140.

[51] Sayers, *The Mind of the Maker*, 26.

[52] Ibid., 23.

[53] Steiner, *Grammars of Creation*, 144.

[54] Chesterton, G.K. *Glass Walking Stick* (London: Methuen and Company, 1955) 182-83.

[55] Hall, *Writing Well*, 25.

[56] Ibid., 30.

[57] Hall, p. 78.

[58] Forde, Nigel. *The Lantern and the Looking-Glass* (London: Society for Prompting Christian Knowledge, 1997) 174.

Chapter Three

[1] Ecclesiastes 3:2-8, New American Standard Version.

[2] Hall, *Writing Well*, 219.

[3] Bogdanovich, *Who the Devil Made It*, 443.

[4] Greenblatt, Stephen. *Will in the World. How Shakespeare Became Shakespeare*. (New York: W. W. Norton and Company, 2004) 295.

[5] Lewis, C.S. "Hamlet–The Prince or the Poem", *Proceedings of the British Academy, XXXVIII* (London: Oxford University Press, 1942) 1415.

[6] Ciment, *Kazan on Kazan*, 110.

[7] Kazan, *My Life*, 500.

[8] Young, Jeff. *Kazan: The Master Director Discusses His Films*. (New York: Newmarket Press, 1999) 117.

[9] Ciment, *Kazan on Kazan*, 87.

[10] Young, *Kazan: The Master Director Discusses His Films*, 124.

[11] Beck, Nicholas. *Budd Schulberg. A Bio-Bibliography* (Lanham, Maryland: The Scarecrow Press, Inc., 2001) 49-50.

[12] Bogdanovich, *Who the Devil Made It*, 421.

[13] Young, *Kazan. The Master Director Discusses His Films*, 171-172.

[14] Dissanayake. *Homo Aestheticus: Where Art Comes from and Why*, 224.

[15] Eibl-Eibesfeldt. *Human Ethology* (New York: Aldine de Gruyter, 1989) 105.

[16] Ibid, 425.

[17] Dissanayake, 225.

[18] No list can be comprehensive. Any list will include these universals: to regulate sex, confer status and role, divide labor by sex and age, socialize children, control disruptive behaviors, distinguish between good and bad conduct, distinguish between effective and ineffective leadership, conceptualize the supernatural, empathize, play with the imagination, use metaphors, fear, hope, love, hate, decorate, use genealogy to determine kinship, perform daily routines, distinguish between self and others, employ symbols, recognize signs, use hands to fight, problem solve by trial and error and insight and reasoning, play games, joke, temper loss, use fire, make tools and containers, trade, consider right and wrong ways to do things, regulate individual actions by the group, form families, use kinship terms, revenge, consider morality, fix responsibility, sense duty and indebtedness, resent, employ causal thinking, have grammatical classes for nouns and verbs, interpret behavior, designate taboo utterances, envy, be ethnocentric, recognize inheritance and succession, settle disputes, avoid

incest, exhibit schizophrenia, use binary distribution, practice reciprocity, give gifts, anthropomorphize, desire children, marry, have values and ideals and standards, recognize property rights, experience boredom and quandaries, sleep, dream, sense affection, submit, feel hostility, care for the ill or injured, prohibit homicide and adultery and untruth, sense pride and shame, act altruistically, sorrow, pay restitution, cook, have mood-altering drugs, prefer faces of average dimensions, employ hairdressing rituals, forget, sense anxiety and solidarity, need privacy and silence, contemplate, lie, ornament, experience grief and loss at the death of kin, create metered poetry, use black and red and white symbolically, set rules of right and wrong, have thirteen semantic primes: *I, you, someone, something, world, this, want, not want, think of, say, imagine, be a part of,* and *become.*

[19] Young, *Kazan: The Master Director Discusses His Films,* 177.

[20] Pope John Paul II, "Letter of His Holiness Pope John Paul II to Artists", 1999.

[21] Neff, David, "The Passion of Mel Gibson" *Christianity Today* Volume 48 Number 2, March 2004, 32.

[22] Young, *Kazan: The Master Director Discusses His Films.* 177.

[23] Bogdanovich, *Who the Devil Made It,* 449.

[24] Ibid., 476.

[25] Ibid., 476-479.

[26] Lissner, Ivar. *Man, God and Magic* (New York: G.P. Putnam's Sons, 1961) 12-13.

27 Armstrong, Karen. *A History of God* (New York: Ballentine Books, 1993) xix.

28 Ibid, 618.

29 Ibid., 631.

30 The terms are used interchangeably in the Bible.

31 Habermas, Gary and Moreland, J.P., *Beyond Death: Exploring the Evidence for Immortality.* (Wheaton, Illinois: Crossway Books, 1998) 70-71.

32 Polkinghorne, John. *Faith, Science, and Understanding* (New Haven: Yale University Press, 2000) 11.

33 Hall, *Writing Well*, 220.

34 Godawa, *Hollywood Worldviews. Watching Films with Wisdom and Discernment*, 17.

Chapter Four

1 Psalm 104: 24, New American Standard Version.

2 Aristotle, *Nicomachean Ethics*, trans. by W.D. Ross, Book VI, Chapter 3, lines 11-13, *The Basic Works of Aristotle* (New York: Random House, 1966).

3 Lissner, *Man, God, and Magic*, 20-21.

4 Vitz, Paul C. *Faith of the Fatherless. The Psychology of Atheism.* (Dallas: Spence Publishing Company, 1999) 3.

5 MacMurray, John. *Persons in Relation.* (Atlantic Heights, N.J.: Humanities Press, Inc., 1961) 155.

6 Psalm 104:30, New American Standard Version.

7 Oden, Thomas C. *The Living God* (Peabody, Ma.: Prince Press: 1987) 152.

[8] Wiesel, Elie, *Talking and Writing and Keeping Silent*, in *The German Church Struggle and the Holocaust*, ed. Franklin H. Littell and Hubert G. Locke (Detroit: Wayne State University Press, 1974) 271.

[9] Scarry, Elaine. *On Beauty and Being Just*. (Princeton, N.J.: Princeton University Press, 1999) 5.

[10] Ibid., 3.

[11] Telford, Kenneth. *Aristotle's Poetics: Translation and Analysis*, 2.

[12] Steiner, *Grammars of Creation*, 173.

[13] Chesterton, G. K., *Generally Speaking* (New York: Dodd, Mead and Company, 1929) 120.

[14] Schulberg, Budd. *Moving Pictures: Memories of a Hollywood Prince* (New York: Stein and Day, 1981) 7.

[15] Ibid., 11.

[16] Beck, *Schulberg. A Bio-Bibliography*, 55.

[17] James 1: 17.

[18] Psalm 104: 30.

[19] Ephesians 1:19-20, New International Version.

[20] Wright, N. T. "The Holy Spirit in the Church". *Fulcrum Conference Islington. Inciting Insight: The Holy Spirit*. April 29, 2005 www.fulcrum-anglican.org.uk/events/2005/inthechurch.cfm.

[21] Ibid.

[22] Lewis, C.S. *Mere Christianity.*, 54.

[23] Oden, Thomas C. *The Living God*, 270.

[24] Wright, "The Holy Spirit in the Church".

[25] Packer, *Knowing God*. 106.

[26] Aquinas, Saint Thomas. *Summa Theologica*, Question LXXIX, Article One, in Pegis, Anton C. Introduction

to Saint Thomas Aquinas (New York: The Modern Library, 1948) 337.

27 1 Corinthians 2:7-8, 12-13, New American Standard Bible.

28 1 Corinthians 3: 18, New American Standard Bible.

29 1 Corinthians 1: 20-21.

30 1 Corinthians 1: 25-26.

31 Pascal *Pensees*, translated by A.J. Krailsheimer (New York: Penguin Books, 1966) 85.

32 Pope John Paul II, "Letter of His Holiness Pope John Paul II to Artists", 1999.

33 1 Corinthians 1: 8.

34 Bonhoeffer, Dietrich. *The Cost of Discipleship*. (New York, Simon and Schuster, 1959) 98.

35 1 Corinthians 4:20.

36 1 Corinthians 4:7.

37 Pascal, *Pensees*, 95.

Chapter Five

1 Pope John Paul II, "Letter of His Holiness Pope John Paul II to Artists", 1999.

2 John of Damascus, "On the Orthodox Faith" Volume II Section 2 in *A Select Library of the Nicene and Post-Nicene Fathers of the Christian Church* (New York: Christian: 1887-1900). Second Series. Volume IX, 18.

3 Hebrews 12: 2-3, New International Version.

4 1 Peter 3:4, New International Version.

[5] Barth, Karl. *Church Dogmatics, III,* 4 (Edinburgh: T and T Clark, 1961) 374-385.

[6] Isaiah 35: 10, Revised Standard Version.

[7] John 16:22, New Living Translation.

[8] Steiner, *Grammars of Creation*, 173.

[9] McLuhan, *The Medium and the Light: Reflections on Religion,* 14.

[10] Chesterton, *Orthodoxy*, Chapter 6.

[11] Pegis, Anton C., editor. *Introduction to Saint Thomas Aquinas*. (New York: The Modern Library, 1948) 572.

[12] Ibid., 576.

[13] Pope John Paul II, "Letter of His Holiness Pope John Paul II to Artists", 1999.

[14] St. Thomas Aquinas, *Summa Theologica*, I-II ae Q27.1.3.

[15] Wright, N. T. "The Holy Spirit in the Church"

[16] Psalm 27:4.

[17] Psalm 90:17.

[18] Psalm 50:2.

[19] Psalm 96:6,9.

[20] Clement of Alexandria, *Stromata* 5 (PG Vol. 25, c. 71.)

[21] Teachout, Terry. *A Terry Teachout Reader* (New Haven: Yale University Press, 2004) xxi-xxii.

[22] Oden, Thomas. *The Living God*, 168.

[23] St. Augustine, *The Confessions*, trans. by R.S.Pine-Coffin (London: Penguin Books, 1961), Book X, Section 34.

[24] Michelangelo Buonarroti, Poem nr. CIX, to Cavaleri.

[25] Schaeffer, Francis A. "How Should We Then Live?" *The Complete Works of Francis A. Schaeffer* (Wheaton, Illinois: Crossway Books, 1982), Volume 5, 203.

[26] Vitruvius, *De Architecture*, III, 1.

[27] Dubay, Thomas. *The Evidential Power of Beauty* (San Francisco, California: Ignatius Press, 1999), 39.

[28] Aristotle, *Metaphysics*, 985 b. 23.

[29] Wilson, *Consilience: The Unity of Knowledge*, 219.

[30] St. Augustine, *City of God* XI, 4.

[31] Yanagi, Mueyoshi. *The Unknowable Craftsman: A Japanese Insight into Beauty by Soetsu Yanagi* (Palo Alto, California: Kodansha International, 1972), 131.

[32] Dubay, *The Evidential Power of Beauty*, 50.

[33] Wright, "The Holy Spirit in the Church".

[34] Von Balthasar, Hans Urs. *The Glory of the Lord* (San Francisco, California: Ignatus Press, 1982-1989) Volume 1,151.

[35] St. Augustine, Book IV, Section 13.

[36] St. Augustine, Book IV, Section 10.

[37] Von Balthasar, *The Glory of the Lord*, 442.

[38] Packer, *Knowing God*, 92.

[39] Keller, Tim. *"Glory"* in *It Was Good. Making Art to the Glory of God.* (Baltimore, Maryland: Square Halo Books, 2000) 81.

[40] Chesterton, *Orthodoxy*. 117.

[41] Pope John Paul II, "Letter of His Holiness Pope John Paul to Artists", 1999.

[42] Deuteronomy 16:15, New International Version.

[43] Steiner, *Grammars of Creation*, 45.

[44] Ibid.,48.

Chapter Six

[1] 2 Timothy 3:1-6, New Living translation.

[2] Phillips, J.B. *When God Was Man* (Nashville, Tennessee: Abingdon Press, 1955) 26-27.

[3] Romans 12:2.

[4] Galatians 5:6.

[5] Hendra, Tony. *Father Joe. The Man Who Saved My Soul.* (New York: Random House, 2004) 202.

[6] Pope John Paul II, "Letter of His Holiness Pope John Paul II to Artists", 1999.

[7] Matthew 22: 37-39.

[8] John 14:23.

[9] Wright, "The Holy Spirit in the Church".

[10] Neff, David. "The Passion of Mel Gibson" *Christianity Today* Volume 48, Number 2, March 2004, 33.

[11] Anker, Roy M, "Lights, Camera, Jesus", *Christianity Today,* Volume 44, Number 6, May 22, 2000, 63.

[12] Pinsky, Mark I., "From Davey and Goliath to Homer and Ned", *Christianity Today* Volume 45, Number 2, February 5, 2001, 33.

[13] Luke 18:27.

[14] Proverbs 3:5-6.

[15] 2 Corinthians 9:8.

[16] Philippians 4:13.

[17] Philippians 4:19.

[18] Isaiah 41:10.

[19] 1 Peter 5:7.

[20] Matthew 11:28-30.

[21] Romans 8:28-30

[22] Romans 8:38-39.

[23] Isaiah 26:3.

[24] Colossians 3:12-15.

[25] 2 Timothy 2: 15, New American Standard Version.

[26] Colossians 4:12.

[27] Hendra, *The Man Who Saved My Soul,* 181-182.

[28] Neff, David. "The Passion of Mel Gibson", *Christianity Today* Volume 48, Number 2, March 2004, 34.

[29] "Interview with Tom Shadyac. Director of Bruce Almighty" in HOLLYWOOD JESUS Newsletter Number 56 Pop Culture From A Spiritual Point of View May 24, 2003 <http://www.hollywoodjesus.com/newsletter056.htm>.

[30] Smietana, Bob. "Putting Big Idea back Together" *Christianity Today* Volume 48, Number 5, May 2004, 46.

[31] Luke 22: 27. New American Standard Version, updated.

[32] Matthew 20-25-30.

[33] "John Wesley-Revival and Revolution", *Church History*, Issue 2 (Carol Stream, Illinois: 1997)

[34] Philippians 3:7-8.

[35] Luther, Martin, *Commentary on Romans*, translated by J. Theodore Mueller (Grand Rapids, Michigan: Kregel Publications, 1976) xiii.

[36] Luke 16:15. New American Standard Version, updated.

[37] 1 John 4:11-12.

[38] Philippians 3:12.

[39] Chesterton, *Orthodoxy*, 123.

[40] Speech by Elia Kazan, Wesleyan University, Middletown, Connecticut, 1973.

[41] "Mel Gibson's Statement in Full", *BBC UK Version*, http://news.bbc.co.uk/1/hi/entertainment/5236124.stm, August 1, 2006.

[42] Isaiah 43:18-19 New International Version. Recovery advocate Martin O'Brien contributed to the insights of this paragraph.

[43] Butt, Howard. *The Velvet Colored Brick* (San Francisco, California: Harper and Row: 1973) 43.

[44] Colossians 4:5-6.

[45] McLuhan, *The Medium and the Light: Reflections on Religion,*. 202.

[46] Smietana, Bob, "Running Out of Miracles", *Christianity Today* Volume 48, Number 5, May 2004, 47.

[47] Philippians 2: 14-16.

[48] 2 Corinthians 10: 17-18.

[49] Philippians 4:13.

[50] Colossians 3:8-10.

[51] Chesterton, *Orthodoxy*, 96.

[52] Philippians 2: 3-5

[53] Peacock, Charlie. "Making Art like a True Artist", *It Was Good. Making Art to the Glory of God*, ed., Ned Bustard (Baltimore, Md.: Square Halo Books, 2000) 118.

[54] Colossians 3:17.

[55] Quoted in Warren, Rick, *The Purpose Driven Life* (Grand Rapids, Michigan: Zondervan, 2002) 269.

[56] Colossians 3: 8-9.

[57] Peacock, "Making Art like a True Artist, 118.

[58] Wright, "The Holy Spirit in the Church."

Index

Printed in the United States
113489LV00001B/76/A